A Comparison

of

Six Major

World Religions

Immy Bloodworth Mahitab

ISBN: 979-8-9914768-1-2

Library of Congress Control Number: 2024920326

Table of Contents

Notes on Translations and Quoted Passages

All translations of the Vedas within this book are reprinted with permission from *The Holy Vedas*, translated by Pandit Satyakam Vidyalankar. Copyright © belongs to Pandit Satyakam Vidyalankar.

All translations of the Upanishads within this book are reprinted with permission from *The Upanishads*, introduced and translated by Eknath Easwaran, Copyright © 2007, Nilgiri Press, Blue Mountain Center of Meditation.

All translations of the Bhagavad Gita within this book are reprinted with permission from *The Bhagavad Gita*, introduced and translated by Eknath Easwaran, Copyright © 2007, Nilgiri Press, Blue Mountain Center of Meditation.

All translations of the Tanakh (also known as the Hebrew Bible or the Old Testament) within this book are from *The Holy Bible*, New

1

Introduction

In the spirit of love, learning, peace, and unity, I have written this book explaining the top six major world religions. One of the most important parts of each chapter, if not the most important part, is the section about virtues. I have included this section to show that all of these religions, though differing in beliefs and rituals, share certain virtues, and they are expressed in beautiful ways by the scriptures of each faith. I hope that this book can lead people to better understand and respect one another by showing that we are not so different morally.

I have organized the list of religions according to secular historical chronology, rather than according to the size of each religion's population. This is because populations are subject to change, whereas history is not. Therefore, the order that the religions are presented in this book is:

Introduction

Hinduism, Judaism, Buddhism, Christianity, Islam, and Sikhism.

The current order of the world religions according to population is, from largest to smallest: Christianity, Islam, Hinduism, Buddhism, Sikhism, and Judaism. I have chosen the top six world religions because their scriptures are more accessible, and they can be quoted easily. I do not intend to discriminate against smaller religions by leaving them out.

An Overview of Each Chapter

Each religion has its own chapter, and each chapter follows the same layout. There is a paragraph introducing the religion, and it presents: the name of the religion; the person who brought the religion; when the religion was founded; where the religion originated; the name of the followers of the religion; how many adhere to the religion; the scripture, or scriptures, of the religion; the language of the religion's scripture(s); and the place of worship for adherents of the religion. (Note that the world population for each religion has been gathered online from the World Population Review.)

Then there is a brief section about the etymology of the religion, followed by a section giving the purpose of life according to the religion.

Next is a description of God based on the scripture(s) of the religion, and I have selected passages that show that God is unanimously viewed by each religion as: One, Infinite, Loving, Light, the Creator, the Sustainer, the All-Powerful, and the All-Knowing. Of course, God has more attributes than these in each religion, but in selecting these seven attributes I hope to summarize aspects of God, inasmuch as they can be, and show that the concept of God is similar in most of the religions.

Thereafter, I give a general history and description of the religion, followed by some significant times throughout the year in the religion, and then a list of seven virtues in the religion: Anger Management, Forgiveness, Gratitude, Humility, Kindness, Love, and Patience.

Lastly, I give a description about the symbol commonly associated with the religion.

Introduction

Towards the end of the book, I have added a chapter in which I attempt to show that the concepts of miracles and spiritual experiences exist in all of the major world religions. This chapter begins with an introduction of the subject and proceeds with a section for each religion in which miracle stories are listed. Then a section about particularly significant miracles follows, and a section about spiritual experiences ends the chapter.

Finally, I want to address a matter that applies to all of the religions mentioned herein. Anyone of any race, ethnicity, or gender is allowed to join any of these religions. One does not have to be an Indian to be a Hindu or an Arab to be a Muslim or have Jewish parents to be a Jew. A Scandinavian person may be a Muslim, an African person may be a Hindu, a Korean person may be a Jew, etc. Whether such diversity is actually common is another matter, but contrary to popular belief, all of these religions (Hinduism, Judaism, Buddhism, Christianity, Islam, Sikhism) accept converts.

Chapter 1: Hinduism

Introduction

Hinduism is the most ancient of the major world religions, with its origins going back thousands of years, and historians are unable to trace precisely when it was founded, but it originated with various *rishis*, or seers, in India. A follower of Hinduism is called a Hindu, and Hindus actually refer to Hinduism as *Sanatana Dharma*, which can be translated as "the Eternal Religion." A follower of Sanatana Dharma is called a Dharmi. Therefore, the terms "Hindu" and "Dharmi" are interchangeable. There are approximately 1.16 billion Hindus in the world. A Hindu place of worship is called a mandir. A Hindu priest, who leads worship at a mandir, is called a pandit or pujari.

Sanatana Dharma has many scriptures, but the most ancient and sacred ones are the Vedas, which are classified into four: Rig, Yajur, Sama, and Atharva. They are voluminous, consisting of hymns that focus on a wide range of spiritual matters. Each Veda is subdivided into four categories: Samhitas, Brahmanas, Aranyakas, and Upanishads. The Upanishads are particularly renowned, as they contain *Vedanta*, which is the culmination of the Vedas. In other words, the Upanishads are the philosophical essence of the Vedas. There are 108 Upanishads, but a select few are considered to be the most important, or "major." Note also that the Rig Veda may have been written as early as approximately 4,000 B.C.E., with all other Hindu scriptures being written later. However, traditional Western scholarship often dates the Rig Veda to as early as 1,500 B.C.E.

Other significant scriptures include the Bhagavad Gita, the Brahma Sutras, and the eighteen Puranas. There are also two well-known epics, or Itihasas, called the Ramayana and the Mahabharata (of which the Bhagavad Gita is technically a part). More scriptures exist, but they are lesser known to many people. The Hindu scriptures are written in Sanskrit, using the script called *Devanagari*.

Overall, Hindu scripture is divided into two categories: *shruti* (that which is heard) and *smriti* (that which is remembered). Of the two, shruti is more authoritative because it came directly from God to various rishis. Smriti, however, was written by different rishis and scholars. Of the many scriptures, the Vedas and their subdivisions are considered to be shruti. By extension, this includes the Upanishads. The Bhagavad Gita, Brahma Sutras, Puranas, and Itihasas are considered to be smriti.

Hindu sages have grouped three particular scriptures together as a comprehensive summary of Vedic philosophy, or Vedanta. These scriptures are the Upanishads, the Bhagavad Gita, and the Brahma Sutras. Collectively, they are known as the Prasthana Traya (also spelled "Prasthanatrayi").

Etymology

The word "Hindu" comes from the Persian pronunciation of the word *Sindhu*, which is the Sanskrit term for the Indus River. Persians viewed

Hindus as people living beyond the Indus River, and Europeans later adopted this pronunciation.

Purpose of Life

The purpose of life according to Sanatana Dharma is to transcend the cycle of reincarnation and unite with God, the Divine Soul. One achieves this goal through prayer, yoga, meditation, and good deeds. If this goal is not reached in this lifetime, the soul continues in the cycle of birth, death, and rebirth.

Description of God

He fashions these worlds and pervades them; He bears many a lapse of ours and helps the pious in countless ways. This He does for the welfare of godly devotees; He works unceasingly. He guides His devotee as the Sun regulates seasons; He is the observer of truth and dispeller of evil forces; He is eternal and omniscient. May He convey His devotees across the turbulent sea of life. (Rig Veda 3:16:4)

God is One, the Lord of men, exceeding far and wide. We observe His holy laws. (Rig Veda 8:25:16)

He is omnipresent and all powerful, He rules over all the three regions, Earth, mid-region and the celestial. His one step is rooted in the deep dark mystery, beyond knowledge of mankind. (Atharva 7:26:4)

He is one and one forever remains alone; believe it. There is no second in God. (Atharva Veda 13:5:20)

The Lord of Love is one. There is indeed no other. He is the inner ruler in all beings. He projects the cosmos from himself, maintains and withdraws it back into himself at the end of time. (Shvetashvatara Upanishad 3:2)

Established in peace, they rise above body-consciousness to the supreme light of the Self. Immortal, free from fear, this Self is Brahman, called the True. (Chandogya Upanishad 8:3:4)

[29]Knowing me as the friend of all creatures, the Lord of the universe, the end of all offerings and all spiritual disciplines, they attain eternal peace. (Bhagavad Gita 5:29)

[26]I know everything about the past, the present, and the future, Arjuna; but there is none who knows me completely. (Bhagavad Gita 7:26)

¹⁸I am the goal of life, the Lord and support of all, the inner witness, the abode of all. I am the only refuge, the one true friend; I am the beginning, the staying, and the end of creation; I am the womb and the eternal seed. (Bhagavad Gita 9:18)

²⁹I look upon all creatures equally; none are less dear to me and none more dear. But those who worship me with love live in me, and I come to life in them. (Bhagavad Gita 9:29)

⁸I am the source from which all creatures evolve. The wise remember this and worship me with loving devotion. ⁹Their thoughts are all absorbed in me, and all their vitality flows to me. Teaching one another, talking about me always, they are happy and fulfilled. ¹⁰To those steadfast in love and devotion I give spiritual wisdom, so that they may come to me. ¹¹Out of compassion I destroy the darkness of their ignorance. From within them I light the lamp of wisdom and dispel all darkness from their lives. (Bhagavad Gita 10:8-11)

¹¹Clothed in celestial garments and covered with garlands, sweet-smelling with heavenly fragrances, he showed himself as the infinite Lord, the source of all wonders, whose face is everywhere. ¹²If a thousand suns were to rise in the heavens at the same time, the blaze

*of their light would resemble the splendor of that
supreme spirit. (Bhagavad Gita 11:11-12)*

These verses from the Vedas, the
Upanishads, and the Bhagavad Gita show that
in Sanatana Dharma God is understood to be
One, Infinite, Loving, Light, the Creator, the
Sustainer, the All-Powerful, and the All-
Knowing. God is often referred to in Sanatana
Dharma as *Brahman* or *Ishvara*. Note that while
Hindu theology may be viewed as monotheistic
at its core, it also has elements of polytheism
and pantheism, which will be mentioned later
in this chapter.

Description of the Religion

Sanatana Dharma teaches that there exists
Brahman, Which is God (or *Ishvara*), the Absolute
Reality, and the Origin of all. It is infinite and
unchanging, consisting of pure consciousness
and being. Brahman can be thought of as having
two aspects: Nirguna Brahman and Saguna
Brahman. Nirguna Brahman is Brahman
without qualities, and it can be experienced but

not described with words. Saguna Brahman is Brahman with qualities, and it can be described.

Brahman manifests through creation, and all beings are inherently a part of It. The concept of separateness from Brahman comes from *Maya*, or Illusion, and it is the creative power of God through which we experience the world. The part of an individual that is Brahman is called *Atman*, or the Self, and it is in a causal body (*karana sharira* – also called a spiritual body), which is in an astral body (*sukshma sharira* – also called a subtle or mental body), which is in the physical body (*sthula sharira*). Atman is an individual's true divine essence.

There exists a myriad of different beings in different realms, and among them, residing in a high realm, are powerful beings known as *devas* and *devis*, or gods and goddesses. Certain gods and goddesses oversee certain functions of the world, and they may be viewed as personified qualities of Brahman. Christianity teaches one God in three forms, but Sanatana Dharma teaches one God in many forms. The most significant of the devas are three, which make up the *Trimurti*: Brahma, the Creator;

Vishnu (also called Narayana), the Preserver; and Shiva (also called Mahadeva), the Destroyer. They are each married to devis, with Brahma's wife being Sarasvati, the goddess of inspiration; Vishnu's wife being Lakshmi, the goddess of prosperity; and Shiva's wife being Parvati, the goddess of fertility, love, and devotion. There is also Shakti, the Goddess, representing power and the feminine aspect of divinity. Manifestations of Shakti include the goddesses Durga and Kaali, who are often depicted as warriors. Indra is the god of thunder and rain, and he is the king of Heaven, although Vishnu rules over even Indra. Other popular gods and goddesses include Ganesh (also called Ganapati), the remover of obstacles; Hanuman, a god of devotion; Surya, the god of the sun; and Murugan (also known as Kartikeya and Skanda), a warrior god. Most of the aforementioned gods and goddesses are more worshipped in modern times. Older gods, who were mentioned in the Vedas, include Indra, Agni, Varuna, Soma, and Savitar. There are also more gods and goddesses mentioned in the Hindu scriptures. Worship of the elemental forces is additionally promoted by the Vedas, and certain deities embody these forces. The elements are five: earth (prithvi), water (jalam), fire (agni), wind (vayu), and sky (akash).

Vishnu has incarnated in physical form several times to help save the world, and two of his most significant incarnations are Rama, the hero of the Ramayana, and Krishna, a character in the Mahabharata whose teachings to his disciple Arjuna are recorded in the Bhagavad Gita.

There are different Hindu sects which, though united in their Vedic origins and acceptance of Hindu scriptures, worship certain gods over others, so some people consider them to be different religions under the name of Sanatana Dharma. Vaishnavism regards Vishnu as the primary deity, Shaivism regards Shiva as the primary deity, and Shaktism regards Shakti as the primary deity. There also exists Smartism, which regards Vishnu, Shiva, Shakti, Ganesh, Surya, and Murugan as primary deities. Smartism originated through the influential saint Adi Shankaracharya (c. 8th century C.E.), who was also the one to distinguish the major Upanishads from the minor Upanishads.

It should also be noted that Hindus do not worship cows as gods, but cows are nevertheless highly revered in Sanatana Dharma because they provide humans with nourishment through their milk. They also represent righteousness in that they take very little but give us milk in abundance. Therefore, cows are not to be eaten or slaughtered, and they are treated with utmost respect.

According to Sanatana Dharma, another type of being that exists is the *asura*. Asuras are often referred to in English as "demons," and in Puranic stories they often oppose the devas. However, not all asuras are necessarily evil. Furthermore, there is no concept of an overall "Devil" in Sanatana Dharma.

Sanatana Dharma teaches that souls reincarnate, which means to be born, die, then reborn, and so on. The cycle of birth, death, and rebirth is called *Samsara*. In between lives, an individual can experience bliss or torment, depending on one's consciousness and deeds.

One can be in *Deva Loka*, the realm of the gods; *Pitri Loka*, the realm of the ancestors; or *Patala*, which is Hell. Then one reincarnates into a physical body.

What keeps an individual tied to Samsara is *karma*, which is a moral law of action and reaction, or cause and effect, based on an individual's thoughts, words, and deeds. Good thoughts, words, and deeds lead to good karma, and bad thoughts, words, and deeds lead to bad karma. Moreover, there is karma on an individual level, karma on a group level, and karma on a planetary level. Karma may also play out in this lifetime, or it may affect one in future incarnations. Bad karma can be cleansed out, and good karma can be accrued, through spiritual activities such as charity, prayer, meditation, selfless service, and various rituals including *puja*, which is worship performed by making offerings of objects to deities. The deities are generally depicted in the form of sacred statues called *murtis*.

Karma can be transcended through meditation and devotion to God, which will eventually shift one's consciousness to perceive reality through the Atman and to be in a state of union with God. Then one will cease to reincarnate, and their consciousness will exist blissfully united with Brahman. This is called *moksha*, or freedom, as one is liberated from Samsara after achieving such a state. Note that the word *yoga* means "union," and it refers to spiritual union with God as well as a path that will lead to that union. There are several different paths of yoga, and they include Karma Yoga, Bhakti Yoga, Jnana Yoga, and Raja Yoga. The yoga that many non-Hindus are familiar with is a set of meditative physical positions called Hatha Yoga, but that is just a component of the path of Raja Yoga. A man who practices yoga is called a *yogi*, and a woman who practices yoga is called a *yogini*. Additionally, one seeking moksha is advised to get the help of a *guru*, which is a selfless, enlightened spiritual mentor. Note also that a *sadhu* is a wandering man who has renounced materialism for spirituality. The female equivalent is a *sadhvi*.

An essential concept in Sanatana Dharma is that of *dharma*, which on an individual level can mean righteousness or true purpose, and on a universal level can mean natural law or universal order. When used to refer to an individual's righteousness, dharma is also one of the four goals in the life of a human being, with the other three goals being *artha*, *kama*, and moksha. Artha refers to the resources that lead to a fulfilling and comfortable life. Kama refers to any type of pleasure or delight. Together, dharma, artha, kama, and moksha are referred to as the *purusharthas*, and dharma is the foundation because without it, artha and kama can become self-destructive.

One topic that should perhaps be explained regarding Sanatana Dharma is the so-called caste system, a concept that is often misinterpreted. In Sanatana Dharma, there are four *varnas*, which might be translated as archetypes, and they refer to one's natural inclinations and inherent abilities. They are:

- **Brahmins**: priests, motivated by knowledge
- **Kshatriyas**: rulers, motivated by power
- **Vaishyas**: merchants, motivated by wealth

- **Shudras**: laborers, motivated by work

People are also organized according to *jati*, which is one's profession and can often be hereditary. The term *caste* was imposed on Hindus by outsiders in an attempt to make sense of varnas and jatis. However, certain people misunderstand the system that Sanatana Dharma provided and use a person's class and method of contributing to society as a means to discriminate against them. Some people are even labeled as *dalits*, or untouchables. This is not what Sanatana Dharma prescribes. Sanatana Dharma teaches unity, love, and service to others.

Sanatana Dharma additionally teaches five things that Hindus avoid (yamas), and ten things that Hindus strive to practice (niyamas).

Yamas:

1. **Ahimsa**: not to commit violence
2. **Satya**: not to lie
3. **Asteya**: not to steal
4. **Brahmacharya**: not to overindulge
5. **Aparigraha**: not to be greedy

Niyamas:

1. **Saucha**: cleanliness
2. **Santosha**: contentedness
3. **Tapas**: discipline
4. **Kshama**: patience
5. **Daya**: compassion
6. **Dana**: generosity
7. **Puja**: worship
8. **Svadhyaya**: diligently studying
9. **Japa**: repeating God's name
10. **Ishvara Pranidhana**: surrendering to God

There are many sacred sites in Sanatana Dharma. The festival of the Kumbha Mela is hosted at either Prayag, Nasik, Ujjain, or Hardwar, once every twelve years. It celebrates the spilling of divine nectar into these sites. Mount Kailash and Benares are sacred because of their ties to Shiva. The Sri Venkateshvara Temple in Tirupati is holy because of its ties to Vishnu, as are the cities of Mathura and Vrindavan. Shakti Peeths are temples throughout India in which Shakti is worshipped. There are also other sacred Hindu sites in India.

A Comparison of Six Major World Religions

The history of Sanatana Dharma is tied to the history of India, which has a vast array of cultures and languages. Hindus believe that many of the stories of the gods and goddesses occurred long before secular chronology.

In Sanatana Dharma, time is considered to be cyclical as opposed to linear. There are four ages, or *yugas*, that continuously repeat in a cycle: Satya Yuga (also known as Krita Yuga), Treta Yuga, Dvapara Yuga, and Kali Yuga. The Satya Yuga is an era of righteousness and harmony, and it lasts for 1,728,000 years. In the Treta Yuga, individuals lose a quarter of their righteousness and harmony, and this yuga lasts for 1,296,000 years. In the Dvapara Yuga, individuals lose another quarter of their righteousness and harmony, and this yuga lasts for 864,000 years. In the Kali Yuga, there is only a quarter of righteousness and harmony left, so it is the darkest yuga, and it lasts 432,000 years. We are currently in the Kali Yuga.

However, the division of time does not end there, as there are cycles within cycles. Four yugas make up one maha yuga, which lasts for 4,320,000 human years. Seventy-one maha yugas make up one manavantara. Fourteen manavantaras make up one kalpa, which is one day of Brahma and is equal to 4,320,000,000 years. Creation is active for one kalpa, and then creation lies in a state of rest or destruction for another kalpa. This kalpa of inaction is called a night of Brahma. One day and one night of Brahma equal one ahotram, which is a complete day of Brahma. There are 360 ahotrams in one year of Brahma, and 100 years of Brahma make up the life of Brahma. Thus, Brahma lives for 311,040,000,000,000 human years. After this period, Brahma dies, the universe is destroyed, and then a new Brahma is born and the cycles start over. And this is just one drop of the vast creation of God, as there are many universes at once, each with its own Brahma.

Significant Times throughout the Year

There are many festivals in Sanatana Dharma, and some notable ones include:

Diwali (also spelled "Divali" or "Dipavali"): Known as the Festival of Lights, this five-day celebration commemorates a tale from the

Ramayana that symbolizes the victory of good over evil.

Holi: This day is New Year's Day according to certain Hindu calendars, although other Hindu calendars differ. The two-day festival commemorates the defeat of a demoness called Holika, and people sprinkle each other with colored water and colored powder.

Navratri: This is a nine-day festival in which Hindus fast and worship Goddess Durga.

Krishna Janmashtami: This day celebrates the birth of Krishna, and Hindus fast on this day.

Maha Shivaratri: This day celebrates the marriage of Shiva to Parvati, and Hindus meditate and fast on this day.

Guru Purnima: This is a night on which Hindus honor their gurus. They also honor the sage Vyasa, who organized the Vedas into four books, wrote the Mahabharata, and wrote the eighteen Puranas.

Hinduism

Virtues in Sanatana Dharma

Anger Management

[2]Do not get angry or harm any living creature, but be compassionate and gentle; show good will to all. (Bhagavad Gita 16:2)

Forgiveness

Behave with others as you would with yourself. Look upon all the living beings as your bosom friends, for in all of them there resides one soul. All are but a part of that Universal Soul. A person who believes that all are his soul-mates and loves them all alike, never feels lonely. The divine qualities of forgiveness, compassion and service will make him lovable in the eyes of all. He will experience intense joy throughout his life. (Yajur Veda 40:6)

Gratitude

[26]Whatever I am offered in devotion with a pure heart – a leaf, a flower, fruit, or water – I accept with joy.

[27]Whatever you do, make it an offering to me — the food you eat, the sacrifices you make, the help you give, even your suffering. [28]In this way you will be freed from the bondage of karma, and from its results both pleasant and painful. Then, firm in renunciation and union, with your heart free, you will come to me. (Bhagavad Gita 9:26-28)

Humility

[5]Not deluded by pride, free from selfish attachment and selfish desire, beyond the duality of pleasure and pain, ever aware of the Self, the wise go forward to that eternal goal. (Bhagavad Gita 15:5)

Kindness

May your heart be full of generosity, kindness and love; may it flow to the down-trodden and make them happy! (Sama Veda 55)

Hinduism

Love

I bless you to be free from malice, to live in concord and harmony with all. Love one another as a cow loves its new-born calf. (Atharva Veda 3:30:1)

[55]They live in wisdom who see themselves in all and all in them, who have renounced every selfish desire and sense craving tormenting the heart. (Bhagavad Gita 2:55)

[22]This supreme Lord who pervades all existence, the true Self of all creatures, may be realized through undivided love. (Bhagavad Gita 8:22)

Patience

[3]Cultivate vigor, patience, will, purity; avoid malice and pride. Then, Arjuna, you will achieve your divine destiny. (Bhagavad Gita 16:3)

The Symbol of the Religion

The symbol that is often associated with Sanatana Dharma is the sound *Aum* (pronounced "Om"), written in Sanskrit. Aum is the primordial sound of creation and the essential vibration of the universe. It additionally represents God and the highest state of consciousness. It is also known as *Pranava*.

Pranava Yoga involves meditating on the sound Aum, which may lead one to achieving higher states of consciousness and spiritual insight. Aum is the combination of three sounds, each representing a different state. The first component, "a," represents the waking state; the second component, "u," represents the dream state; and the third component "m," represents the state of deep, dreamless sleep. Thus, Aum represents all states of consciousness, and they are all encapsulated in the fourth state of consciousness, called Turiya, which is pure consciousness. Turiya is symbolized by the silence following the chant. In summary, Aum symbolizes divinity, past, present, and future, and it is the sound of creation itself. Therefore, chanting Aum is believed to bring unity with Brahman.

Hinduism

[1]*Aum stands for the supreme Reality. It is a symbol for what was, what is, and what shall be. Aum represents also what lies beyond past, present, and future. (Mandukya Upanishad, Verse 1)*

Chapter 2: Judaism

Introduction

Judaism is the religion that was initially brought by Abraham in Canaan, and centuries later it was formalized through Moses (c. 1200 B.C.E.) at Mount Sinai near Egypt. As Judaism is exceedingly ancient, it is difficult to date the setting of its founding with historical precision. A follower of Judaism is called a Jew, and there are approximately 14.6 million Jews in the world. The Jewish scriptures are the Tanakh, referred to in English as the Hebrew Bible, and the Talmud. The Tanakh is made up of different books, and the first five books of the Tanakh are collectively referred to as the Torah, which is the most sacred scripture of Judaism. The Torah is also called the Pentateuch or the Five Books of Moses. The Tanakh is written in Hebrew, with some small parts in Aramaic. The Talmud is written in Aramaic, with some portions in Hebrew. The place of worship for Jews is called a synagogue. A

Jewish scholar is called a rabbi, and rabbis are the spiritual leaders of Jewish congregations.

Etymology

The words "Judaism" and "Jew" come from the Hebrew name Judah, which was the name of one of the twelve Israelite tribes, named after its patriarch, Judah son of Israel. In Hebrew, the name is Yehudah, and it comes from the Hebrew word *lehodot*, which means "to thank," as Leah, Yehudah's mother, was thankful at his birth.

Purpose of Life

The purpose of life according to Judaism is to fulfill the sacred honor and privilege of adhering to God's commandments (in Hebrew: *mitzvot*), thereby ensuring one's prosperity in this world and in the life of the World to Come.

<u>Description of God</u>

³⁵*You were shown these things so that you might know that the Lord is God; besides him there is no other. (Tanakh: Deuteronomy 4:35)*

⁴*Hear, O Israel: The Lord our God, the Lord is one. (Tanakh: Deuteronomy 6:4)*

³*Do not keep talking so proudly or let your mouth speak such arrogance, for the Lord is a God who knows, and by him deeds are weighed. (Tanakh: 1 Samuel 2:3)*

¹⁰*"You are my witnesses," declares the Lord, "and my servant whom I have chosen, so that you may know and believe me and understand that I am he. Before me no god was formed, nor will there be one after me. ¹¹I, even I, am the Lord, and apart from me there is no savior." (Tanakh: Isaiah 43:10-11)*

¹⁷*Ah, Sovereign Lord, you have made the heavens and the earth by your great power and outstretched arm. Nothing is too hard for you. (Tanakh: Jeremiah 32:17)*

²*The Lord is my light and my salvation – whom shall I fear? The Lord is the stronghold of my life – of whom shall I be afraid? (Tanakh: Psalm 27:2)*

Judaism

⁴You are radiant with light, more majestic than mountains rich with game. (Tanakh: Psalm 76:4)

⁵You, Lord, are forgiving and good, abounding in love to all who call to you. (Tanakh: Psalm 86:5)

²Before the mountains were born or you brought forth the whole world, from everlasting to everlasting you are God. (Tanakh: Psalm 90:2)

²Why do the nations say, "Where is their God?" ³Our God is in heaven; he does whatever pleases him. (Tanakh: Psalm 115:2-3)

⁵Great is our Lord and mighty in power; his understanding has no limit. (Tanakh: Psalm 147:5)

⁶You alone are the Lord. You made the heavens, even the highest heavens, and all their starry host, the earth and all that is on it, the seas and all that is in them. You give life to everything, and the multitudes of heaven worship you. (Tanakh: Nehemiah 9:6)

These verses from the Tanakh show that in Judaism God is understood to be One, Infinite, Loving, Light, the Creator, the Sustainer, the All-Powerful, and the All-Knowing. The name of God in Judaism is considered to be unpronounceable, and it is represented by the

Tetragrammaton, which consists of four Hebrew letters, the equivalents of which in English are YHWH. In place of this name, Jews often refer to God as *Adonai*, Lord; or *HaShem*, The Name. *Elohim* is another word for God.

History and Description of the Religion

God created Adam and Eve, the first man and woman, and He placed them in the Garden of Eden. God forbade them to eat from a certain tree, but a serpent convinced Eve to eat from the tree, and she had Adam eat from the tree as well. Thereafter, God cast them all out of the Garden of Eden, and God gave Adam six laws. After generations came and went, Adam's descendants, humanity, became corrupt on the Earth, so God sent a flood to wipe them out. However, God had warned Noah, the most righteous of his generation, and he built a large boat called an ark, putting in it his family and at least two of every animal. Noah was thereby saved, and when the flood waters receded and Noah disembarked, God gave Noah a seventh law to add to the six He had given to Adam.

These laws are referred to as the seven Noahide Laws, and Jews view them as binding upon all humanity, as all humanity would from then on be descended from Noah.

One of Noah's descendant's, Abram, migrated to the land of Canaan. Abram was so righteous that God changed his name to Abraham and made a covenant with him in which God would give to Abraham's descendants through his son Isaac, and through Isaac's son Jacob, the land of Canaan. For their part of the covenant, Abraham, and the males of his family and descendants, would be circumcised. Abraham, Isaac, and Jacob were all righteous men, and God also gave Jacob the name Israel. Israel had twelve sons, and one of them, Joseph, ended up in a prominent position in Egypt after a series of trying events. There was also a famine in Canaan at that time, so Israel and his family migrated to Egypt to be with Joseph. Each of Israel's twelve sons would become the patriarch of a tribe.

In Egypt, the population of the Children of Israel, also known as the Israelites, grew over the centuries until they were a nation. The Egyptians began to enslave the Israelites, subjecting them to persecution and heavy labor. But God sent an Israelite named Moses, along with his brother Aaron, with miracles to show to people that they were from God. Moses confronted the pharaoh of that time, known throughout history simply as Pharaoh, telling him to allow the Israelites to go with Moses so they could worship God, but Pharaoh was arrogant, and he refused, despite the miracles. God thereupon sent ten plagues in succession on the Egyptians, and afterwards Moses led the Israelites out of that country, an event known as the *Exodus*. Pharaoh and his forces pursued them, but at the Sea of Reeds the waters miraculously parted, allowing the Israelites to cross unharmed, and the waters came down on Pharaoh and his forces, drowning them.

God then led Moses and the Israelites to Mount Sinai, also called Mount Horeb, where He made a covenant with them through the *Ten Statements*, often translated as the Ten Commandments. According to Jewish tradition, all of the Israelites heard the first two statements from God, and then, at their request, Moses transmitted to them the rest of the eight. Moses then ascended the mountain, and there the Ten Statements were written on two stone tablets. Moses also received the *Torah*, meaning the "Teaching," from God. It contained 613 commandments that would be binding on the Israelites for the rest of time. The 613 commandments were summarized in the form of the Ten Statements. It should be noted that Moses received the Torah in two versions, one written and the other oral, and the two versions complemented each other. A high priesthood was also established through Aaron and his descendants. Thereafter, Moses led the Israelites toward Canaan, but most of the Israelites refused to enter it because of the might of the Canaanites. Therefore, God condemned the Israelites to wander the wilderness for forty years. During that time, Moses and the Israelites conquered lands east of the Jordan River. After the death of Moses, his successor Joshua conquered Canaan, which was west of the Jordan River, and Canaan became the home of the Israelites. Over time, the Israelites had conflicts with neighboring nations, and the Israelites were ruled by leaders called judges.

Generations after Joshua, the last judge was named Samuel, and God appointed a king over the Israelites through him. The king was named

Saul, but he became corrupt, so God, through Samuel, gave the kingship to a righteous man named David, and the kingship was to remain through David's descendants from then on. Also, a descendant of Aaron, named Zadok, became the high priest, and the high priesthood would remain through Zadok's descendants. David's son, King Solomon, who was a very wise man, built the Temple in the city of Jerusalem, which would become the holiest place of worshipping God for the Israelites. After Solomon, the kingdom of Israel split into two parts, with the northern kingdom retaining the name Israel and the southern kingdom, which had Jerusalem and was ruled by David's descendants, being called Judah, after the ruling tribe. An individual from Judah was known as a Jew. Over the centuries, most of the Israelites continually disobeyed God and rejected the Torah, and God continually sent people who received inspiration from Him, called *prophets*, to guide them. One notable prophet was Elijah, who preached against worshipping a false god named Baal. Elijah, without having died, was taken up in a whirlwind and a fiery chariot, and it is predicted in the Tanakh that Elijah will someday return. Eventually, the Assyrian Empire conquered and scattered the northern kingdom in 722 B.C.E., and the Babylonian Empire conquered the southern kingdom in 586 B.C.E., destroying the Temple in Jerusalem.

The Babylonians exiled the upper class Jews to Babylon and effectively ended the Davidic monarchy. The Babylonian Exile lasted for about 70 years until the Babylonians were conquered by the Persian Achaemenid emperor, Cyrus, who allowed the Jews to return to Judah and rebuild their Temple. This return to Judah was led by the Torah scholar Ezra, who revived the religion and led a council of 120 prophets and sages called the Great Assembly, and they formalized aspects of the Jewish religion, such as how to pray and what books after the Torah were considered sacred. From then on, prophets ceased to be sent, and the Israelites were spiritually led by scholars called *rabbis*.

Over time, the Jews lived under the Achaemenid Persian Empire, then Alexander III of Macedon, then the Ptolemaic Egyptians, then the Seleucid Empire. A Seleucid king named Antiochus IV Epiphanes persecuted the Jews, but a Jewish family known as the Maccabees, also known as the Hasmoneans, led a successful revolt against the Seleucids and established a kingdom led by the Hasmonean Dynasty. During the time of the Hasmoneans, the Zadokite high priesthood in Jerusalem ended. Eventually, the Romans gained power in the region and formally annexed Judah, which they called Judea. The Parthians very briefly conquered and ruled Judea, but the Romans expelled the Parthians and regained control. The Hasmonean Dynasty ended around that time, and the Romans appointed rulers over Judea.

At this time there existed different Jewish sects: the Pharisees, the Sadducees, and the Essenes. One of the most prominent rabbis, named Hillel, was from the Pharisee sect, and his school of thought established many influential rulings based on the Torah. After the time of Hillel, the Jews revolted against Roman rule in 66 C.E. In the year 70 C.E., the Romans destroyed the Second Temple, and in the year 73 C.E. the Great Revolt ended. Around this time, all of the Jewish sects died out except for the Pharisee sect, which evolved into what is known as Rabbinic Judaism. Over the next few decades there would be two more failed Jewish rebellions against the Roman Empire: the Kitos War and the Bar Kokhba Revolt. The Romans would rename the land of Judea to Palestine. There is debate as to when the books of the Hebrew Bible were finished being canonized by rabbis, but some suggest it was as late as the 2nd century C.E.

Due to the concern of the previous persecution of the Jews, as well as their scattering around the world, rabbis decided to write down the Oral Torah in the form of scholarly discussions about it, and this work became known as the *Mishnah*. It was codified by Rabbi Judah HaNasi (that is, Judah the Prince) in 190 C.E. Commentaries on the Mishnah called *Gemaras* would be written by rabbis over the next few centuries, and they were completed by 600 C.E. There are two Gemaras: a Jerusalem Gemara and a Babylonian Gemara, composed in those respective lands, and it is the Babylonian one that is more widely used by Jews. The Mishnah along with the Gemara is known as the *Talmud*.

A Comparison of Six Major World Religions

Over the centuries, there evolved different forms of Rabbinic Judaism. The Sephardi, Ashkenazi, and Mizrahi differ culturally but not theologically. Within Ashkenazi Judaism, there are the Orthodox, Conservative, and Reform sects. They differ based on their interpretations of Jewish law (in Hebrew: *Halakhah*) as well as their beliefs about whether the Torah was authored by God or humans. There is also a very liberal fourth sect called Reconstructionism, and it has a more abstract view of God. Additionally, there exists Karaite Judaism, which differs from Rabbinic Judaism in that it rejects the Talmud, but Karaite Jews are now a very small minority.

Judaism teaches that eventually there will be a Jewish man with the title of *Mashiach*, or *Messiah* in English, which means "Anointed." The Messiah will be a just ruler and a direct descendant of David and Solomon through the paternal line. During the age of the Messiah, the Israelites will return to their land from throughout the world, the Temple will be rebuilt in Jerusalem for a third time, there will be worldwide peace, all the Jews will adhere to the Torah, and there will be a universal knowledge of God amongst all peoples.

Many Jews believe that after the Messiah comes, those of humanity who have died will be resurrected and allowed to experience an existence of peace, both Jew and Gentile (non-Jew), if they were righteous. The wicked among humanity will not be resurrected. This concept is known as *Olam HaBah*, the World to Come. Olam HaBah may also refer to the afterlife in general, the nature about which different Jews hold different opinions.

Jews also believe in *angels*, which are spiritual beings that act as messengers of God, worship Him, and perform various tasks that He assigns to them. Angels cannot disobey God, and four particularly important angels in Judaism are Michael, the angel who expresses God's kindness; Gabriel, the angel who expresses God's severity; Raphael, the angel of healing; and Uriel, the angel who delivers knowledge of God to people. These four angels surround the throne of God. There also exists an angel named Satan, whose name means "Adversary" or "Prosecutor," and his task is to tempt humans to do evil, thereby testing whether they will choose good. This allows people to grow spiritually by earning their virtue. Jews believe that Satan is not evil or fallen, and he is simply an angel doing what God commands him to do.

Regarding Jewish beliefs, the great Jewish scholar Maimonides (1138 – 1204 C.E.) came up with thirteen principles that are widely accepted by Jews today. They are, in summary:

1. God exists.

2. God is one and unique.

3. God is incorporeal (meaning immaterial, or without a physical body).

4. God is eternal.

5. Prayer is to be directed to God alone and to no other.

6. The words of the prophets are true.

7. Moses was the greatest of the prophets; his prophecies are true.

8. Moses received the Written Torah and the Oral Torah.

9. There will be no other Torah.

10. God knows the thoughts and deeds of humans.

11. God will reward the good and punish the wicked.

12. The Messiah will come.

13. The dead will be resurrected.

Regarding Jewish practices, there are 613 commandments in the Torah that are incumbent upon Jews, but these 613 commandments can each be classified according to one of the Ten Statements (in Hebrew: *Aseret HaDibrot*). Therefore, the Ten Statements will be presented here as they appear in the Torah, in Exodus, Chapter 20:

1. I am the Lord your God, who brought you out of Egypt, out of the land of slavery.

2. You shall have no other gods before me. You shall not make for yourself an image in the form of anything in heaven above or on the earth beneath

or in the waters below. You shall not bow down to them or worship them; for I, the Lord your God, am a jealous God, punishing the children for the sin of the parents to the third and fourth generation of those who hate me, but showing love to a thousand generations of those who love me and keep my commandments.

3. You shall not misuse the name of the Lord your God, for the Lord will not hold anyone guiltless who misuses his name.

4. Remember* the Sabbath day by keeping it holy. Six days you shall labor and do all your work, but the seventh day is a sabbath to the Lord your God. On it you shall not do any work, neither you, nor your son or daughter, nor your male or female servant, nor your animals, nor any foreigner residing in your towns. For in six days the Lord made the heavens and the earth, the sea, and all that is in them, but he rested on the seventh day.

Therefore the Lord blessed the Sabbath day and made it holy.

5. Honor your father and your mother, so that you may live long in the land the Lord your God is giving you.

6. You shall not murder.

7. You shall not commit adultery.

8. You shall not steal.

9. You shall not give false testimony against your neighbor.

10. You shall not covet your neighbor's house. You shall not covet your neighbor's wife, or his male or female servant, his ox or donkey, or anything that belongs to your neighbor.

*Note that the Ten Statements are given again in Deuteronomy, Chapter 5, and there it says to "observe the Sabbath day," instead of to "remember" it. Jews believe that God spoke both commands, and for this reason two candles are traditionally lit before the Sabbath starts – one to symbolize remembering it and one to symbolize observing it. Also note that the Hebrew word for Sabbath is *Shabbat*, and the Sabbath is on Saturday.

Within the Torah, there are dietary laws that Jews must keep. A food or drink that is permissible for a Jew to consume is called *kosher*, which means "fit."

According to the Torah, if the Jews keep the commandments of God, then things will go well for them in this world, and they will be prosperous. If, however, they abandon God's commandments, then their affairs in this world will be bleak.

The following are the seven Noahide Laws, which Jews believe are binding upon all of humanity:

1. Establish courts of laws.

2. Do not curse the name of God.

3. Do not worship idols.

4. Do not engage in forbidden sexual practices.

5.   Do not shed blood.

6.   Do not commit theft.

7.   Do not eat flesh from an animal that is still alive.

The sources for these laws are in the Talmud, in Sanhedrin 56a and in Tosefta Avodah Zarah 8:4.

Note that according to Maimonides, in Laws of Kings 9:4, the command to establish courts of laws is meant to enforce the other six Noahide commands. Note also that there are six types of forbidden sexual practices, as mentioned in Maimonides's Laws of Kings 9:5, and they are: sex with one's mother, with one's father's wife, with another man's wife, with one's sister from the same mother, with a male in a homosexual union, and with an animal. However, certain Jews have varying interpretations of the laws and allow acts like homosexuality.

Significant Times throughout the Year

There are many sacred times in Judaism, other than the weekly Sabbath, and they include:

Rosh Hashanah: This is the Jewish New Year, and it takes place on the 1st of the Hebrew month of Tishri.

Yom Kippur (the Day of Atonement): This is the holiest day of the year in Judaism, when Jews believe that they are closest to God. They spend the day solemnly praying and fasting to atone for their sins.

Sukkot (the Festival of Booths): This is a seven-day celebration of the fall harvest that takes place on the fifth day after Yom Kippur, and it also commemorates when the Israelites were wandering in the wilderness for forty years and living in temporary shelters, or "booths." This forty-year period took place in between the Exodus from Egypt and the Conquest of Canaan.

Chanukah (also spelled "Hanukkah"): This is an eight-day festival commemorating the rededication of the Temple to God after it was defiled under the reign of Antiochus IV Epiphanes.

Purim: This is a festival commemorating a story found in the Book of Esther, which is in the Hebrew Bible. In that story, which takes place during the reign of the Achaemenid Persian Empire, two Jewish figures named Esther and Mordecai foil the plot of the king's official, Haman, in which the Jews are to be exterminated.

Pesach (Passover): This celebrates the beginning of the harvest season in the spring, and it also commemorates a story from the Torah in which God passed over, or spared, the houses of the Israelites when He caused the firstborn of each Egyptian to die. This was in retribution for the Egyptians oppressing the Israelites.

Shavuot (the Festival of Weeks): This celebrates the harvesting of the first fruits as well as when God gave the Torah to Moses at Mount Sinai.

Tisha B'Av: This is the 9th day of the Hebrew month of Av, and it commemorates the destruction of the Jewish Temple in Jerusalem, as well as other tragedies that have befallen the Jewish people throughout history. It is said that the First Temple was destroyed by the

Babylonians on the 9th of Av, and the Second Temple was destroyed by the Romans also on the 9th of Av. This is a solemn day of mourning and fasting for Jews around the world. It may also be noted that if Tisha B'Av falls on a Saturday (Shabbat), its observance is postponed to Sunday.

Virtues in Judaism

Anger Management

28Like a city whose walls are broken through is a person who lacks self-control. (Tanakh: Proverbs 25:28)

Forgiveness

2Speak to the entire assembly of Israel and say to them: 'Be holy because I, the Lord your God, am holy. (Tanakh: Leviticus 19:2)

38Yet he was merciful; he forgave their iniquities and did not destroy them. Time after time he restrained his anger and did not stir up his full wrath. (Tanakh: Psalm 78:38)

Judaism

Gratitude

[10]When you have eaten and are satisfied, praise the Lord your God for the good land he has given you. (Tanakh: Deuteronomy 8:10)

Humility

[12]Before a downfall the heart is haughty, but humility comes before honor. (Tanakh: Proverbs 18:12)

Kindness

[8]He has shown you, O mortal, what is good. And what does the Lord require of you? To act justly and to love mercy and to walk humbly with your God. (Tanakh: Micah 6:8)

[9]This is what the Lord Almighty said: 'Administer true justice; show mercy and compassion to one another. [10]Do not oppress the widow or the fatherless, the foreigner or the poor. Do not plot evil against each other.' (Tanakh: Zechariah 7:9-10)

[21]Whoever pursues righteousness and love finds life, prosperity and honor. (Tanakh: Proverbs 21:21)

55

Love

¹⁸Do not seek revenge or bear a grudge against anyone among your people, but love your neighbor as yourself. I am the Lord. (Tanakh: Leviticus 19:18)

³³When a foreigner resides among you in your land, do not mistreat them. ³⁴The foreigner residing among you must be treated as your native-born. Love them as yourself, for you were foreigners in Egypt. I am the Lord your God. (Tanakh: Leviticus 19:33-34)

Patience

⁸The end of a matter is better than its beginning, and patience is better than pride. (Tanakh: Ecclesiastes 7:8)

The Symbol of the Religion

The symbol that is often associated with Judaism is the Magen David, the Shield of David, more commonly known as the Star of David. While it is supposed to represent David's shield, there is no mention of it in early rabbinic literature or in the Hebrew Bible, and it came into use during the Middle Ages. There are various interpretations as to what the star symbolizes. Some say that its six points represent David being protected by God on all six sides. Some say that the six points of the star represent six days of the week, and the core of it is the sabbath day. Some say that the triangle pointing upwards represents the Israelites' relationship with God, and the triangle pointing downwards represents God's relationship with the Israelites. Some say that the twelve sides of the star represent the twelve tribes of Israel, and the core of the star represents God.

Chapter 3:
Buddhism

Introduction

Buddhism is the religion that emerged from the teachings of Siddhartha Gautama (c. 563 – c. 483 B.C.E.), known as the Buddha, around the year 528 B.C.E. in North India. A follower of Buddhism is called a Buddhist, and there are approximately 507 million Buddhists in the world. The Buddhist scriptures include the Tripitaka, which is Sanskrit for the "Three Baskets." The Baskets, or *Pitakas*, are the Vinaya Pitaka, the Sutta Pitaka, and the Abhidhamma Pitaka. Collectively, they are called the Pali Canon, and the Pali word for the Tripitaka is "Tipitaka." The Buddhist scriptures also include the Sutras, the Shastras, and the Tantras. There is a particularly popular collection of the Buddha's sayings from the Tripitaka that is called the Dhammapada. It is specifically a part of the Sutta Pitaka. The Tripitaka is written in Pali, and the Sutras, Shastras, and Tantras are written in Sanskrit.

Etymology

The keyword in Buddhism is *buddha*, and the word "buddha" means "fully awakened one." It comes from the Sanskrit word *budh*, which means "to awaken."

Purpose of Life

The purpose of life according to Buddhism is to live a moral and mindful life in order to attain a cessation of ego and suffering called *Nirvana*, thereby transcending the cycle of birth, death, and rebirth. If one does not attain this goal, then one will reincarnate into another body or form of being.

Concept of God

In Buddhism, there is no concept of God as there is in theistic religions. The Buddha neither denied nor affirmed the existence of God, so many Buddhists neither believe nor disbelieve in God. Rather, the concept of God is viewed as irrelevant to living a moral life and attaining the spiritual state of Nirvana. God, as understood in other religions, is not discernable, according to Buddhism.

The Buddha said this: "Mendicants, transmigration (i.e., the cycle of birth, death, and rebirth) has no known beginning. No first point is found of sentient beings roaming and transmigrating, shrouded by ignorance and fettered by craving. (Tripitaka: Sutta Pitaka: Samyutta Nikaya 15:1)

(The Buddha said:) "So it seems that none of those brahmins (i.e., Hindu priests and scholars) have seen Brahma (i.e., God) with their own eyes, and not even the ancient seers claimed to know where he is. Yet the brahmins proficient in the Vedas say: 'We teach the path

*to the company of that which we neither know nor
see. This is the only straight path, the direct route that
delivers one who practices it to the company of Brahma.'
What do you think, Vasettha? This being so, doesn't
their statement turn out to have no demonstrable basis?"*

*(Vasettha said:) "Clearly that's the case, Master
Gautama."*

*(The Buddha said:) "Good, Vasettha. For it is
impossible that they should teach the path to that which
they neither know nor see." (Tripitaka: Sutta Pitaka:
Digha Nikaya: Silakkhandha Vagga 13)*

History and Description of the Religion

Buddhists believe in the concept of
reincarnation, a doctrine in which one is born,
dies, is reborn, and so on. This cycle of birth,
death, and rebirth is known as *Samsara*.
Additionally, one may be born into this world
or into other worlds or realms of existence.
Within this realm, the Realm of Desire, there
are heavenly dimensions and hellish
dimensions, and people can be reborn as gods,
titans, humans, animals, hungry ghosts, or

denizens of hell. Besides the Realm of Desire, there also exists the Realm of Form and the Realm of No-Form.

On the subject of different realms and beings, there is no concept of an overall "Devil" in Buddhism. Some may equate the concept of Mara, the Tempter, to the concept of the Devil. However, such a comparison may be viewed as an oversimplification or even a distortion. In Buddhism, Mara is largely regarded as symbolic of selfish passion within all of us.

Where we end up all depends on our *karma*. Karma is essentially the returning force of one's *intentional* thoughts, words, and actions. For example: if one intentionally does good, good will come to that person; but if one intentionally does bad, bad will come to that person. This does not mean that bad things will not happen to good people, or that good things will not happen to bad people, but whatever we do will eventually come back to us somehow, in some way, in this lifetime or another.

Buddhism

Desire is what binds us to reincarnating in this world again and again. When one becomes attached to worldly things, one will keep coming back to the world. The ultimate goal of a Buddhist is to transcend Samsara, thereby transcending the suffering it causes.

Unlike most religions, Buddhism has an impersonal, rather than a personal, concept of "being." Hindus believe in the concept of Atman, Self, which is essentially one's true Self – the part of one that is the Absolute Reality. Opposite to that, Buddhists believe in *Anatman*, No-Self, which is essentially that there is no such thing as one's true Self – there is just Absolute Reality, beyond all desire. In a way, it can therefore be said that Buddhists do not embrace the perspective of having a soul insofar as the soul is a personal divine connection or divinity. But Buddhists do accept the concept of the soul insofar as the soul is merely one's thoughts and deeds.

The state of totally annihilating the concept of the self, resulting in just blissfully being, is known as *Nirvana*, which means "extinguished." In English, it is often used synonymously with the term "enlightenment." Nirvana is not a physical place but a state of being. It is the cessation of lust, hatred, and delusion. When one who has attained Nirvana dies, they then attain *Parinirvana*, the state of Nirvana without a body.

It should also be noted that Buddhists typically do not identify with any sort of personal deity, nor do they worship the Buddha as a deity.

Buddhism is essentially founded in what are known as the *Three Jewels*, and a Buddhist is one who takes refuge in the Three Jewels. This is not necessarily a divine refuge, but a source of guidance and stability. The Three Jewels of Buddhism are:

1. The Buddha
2. The Dharma
3. The Sangha

Jewel 1: The Buddha

Siddhartha Gautama was born around the year 563 B.C.E., although there are different opinions about the exact year of his birth. His father was a leader of the Sakya tribe on the border of northern India and southern Nepal.

Buddhism

A prophecy was told to his father, predicting that Siddhartha would become either a ruler of the kingdom or an enlightened man. Desiring the former, his father sheltered his son from the outside world and kept him in comfort, showering him with worldly pleasures. Nevertheless, Siddhartha grew into a compassionate and reflective young man, who did not succumb to vanity. He was soon married and had a son. The king could not hold his son, Siddhartha, within the palace walls forever, and Siddhartha eventually took trips outside the palace grounds, where he witnessed four things that changed his view of the world: an old man, a maimed man, a corpse in a funeral procession, and a monk.

Following the experiences, Siddhartha decided to leave his royal home and become a wandering ascetic, devoting all of his time to finding the truth, the way to freedom from suffering. He heard and rejected the teachings of certain Hindu priests, moving on to join a band of ascetics who believed that through extreme self-mortification, one could attain enlightenment. After spending some time with them, Siddhartha found that there was nothing to be gained in their techniques, and after abandoning them he eventually sat under a fig tree and meditated, conquering his worldly desires. It was under that tree that Siddhartha attained enlightenment, and he became a buddha, as others had become buddhas long ago. He had found the path to transcend suffering and to attain Nirvana, based on seeing the impermanent, painful, and not-self nature of experience and so relinquishing attachment to the world and self-centered thoughts and behaviors. Universal compassion and loving kindness are the natural results of this release, and these qualities shone forth through the Buddha's character. He thereafter devoted the rest of his life to selflessly spreading his knowledge, and he gained a large, devoted following. The Buddha passed away, attaining Parinirvana, at the age of 80.

Jewel 2: The Dharma

In Buddhism, the Dharma refers to all Buddhist teachings and all that is virtuous, the foundations of which are the Four Noble Truths:

Buddhism

1. All life is *duhkha*. (Duhkha is usually translated as "suffering," but it can also mean "impermanence" or "imperfection." Even worldly happiness is a form of duhkha because it can easily be spoiled, and pain will follow.)

2. The cause of suffering (duhkha) is desire.

3. Suffering can end if one lays aside their desires.

4. The way to end suffering is following the Eightfold Path, also known as the Middle Way because it avoids the opposite extremes of self-indulgence and self-mortification:

    1) **Right Understanding**: To see things as they are, without bias.

    2) **Right Thought**: To have good intentions and compassion toward all beings.

3) **Right Speech**: To think before you speak, and to restrain your tongue to avoid causing offense.

4) **Right Action**: To do nothing that will cause unnecessary harm to others.

5) **Right Livelihood**: To earn a living through helpful and moral methods.

6) **Right Effort**: To have a good attitude and determination towards living well.

7) **Right Mindfulness**: To be entirely in the moment, with no stray thoughts or judgment, and to observe everything you do.

8) **Right Concentration**: To practice meditation, which will increase one's stillness.

Jewel 3: The Sangha

For many people, the Sangha is essentially the Buddhist community, and it can provide a practicing Buddhist with spiritual encouragement. For other people, who are more traditional in their views, the Sangha applies only to Buddhist monastics.

The Precepts

All Buddhists adhere to a set of moral guidelines known as the 5 Precepts, which are:

1. Do not destroy life.

2. Do not steal.

3. Do not commit sexual misconduct.

4. Do not lie.

5. Do not take intoxicants.

Monks, who choose to seclude themselves from regular society in stricter pursuit of their religious endeavors, have additional precepts they must adhere to. Common additional monastic precepts are:

1. Do not take food from noon to the next morning.

2. Do not adorn the body with anything other than the monk's robe.

3. Do not participate in, or watch, public entertainments.

4. Do not use comfortable beds.

5. Do not use money.

The History of the Buddhist Scriptures and Sects

Soon after the death of the Buddha, five hundred of his followers held the Council of Rajagriha to orally canonize and memorize the Buddha's teachings. About 100 years later, seven hundred enlightened Buddhists held the Council of Vesali to debate certain teachings of the Buddha. Thereafter, two Buddhist sects formed: Theravada and Mahayana. Theravada Buddhism places a greater emphasis on monasticism, which means renouncing the world and living as a monk or a nun, as the path to Nirvana. In Theravada, there is also a focus on rules and studying scriptures, and the ideal enlightened individual is called an *arhat*.

Mahayana Buddhism promotes the idea that all individuals, monastics and laypeople, can successfully pursue the path to Nirvana. Mahayana also emphasizes intuition, and the ideal enlightened individual is called a *bodhisattva*. Bodhisattvas are believed to reincarnate in order to help others to transcend Samsara, and they can delay their own final enlightenment (Parinirvana) in order to accomplish this.

After about 135 years, an Indian ruler, King Ashoka, converted to Buddhism and promoted its spread to different regions. He held the Council of Pataliputra, which consisted of one thousand Buddhist monks, and this council again reviewed the Buddha's teachings.

Eventually, in the 1st century B.C.E., the Council of Sri Lanka was held, in which the Buddha's teachings were written down in the form of the *Tripitaka*, also known as the Pali Canon. Although the Mahayana Buddhists accept the Tripitaka, they believe that in the 1st century C.E. more teachings were canonized at the Council of Jalandhar, held by the North Indian king, Kanishka. The Mahayana Buddhists regard the Council of Jalandhar as the fourth council, and it would lead to the creation of the Mahayana scriptures: the *Sutras*, the *Shastras*, and the *Tantras*.

Additionally, another more esoteric sect of Buddhism, called Vajrayana, had evolved from Mahayana by the 3rd century B.C.E. It focuses on symbols, rituals, and deities. Vajrayana has flourished in Tibet, among other places, and the Dalai Lama is a Tibetan Buddhist leader that is viewed as the reincarnation of a great bodhisattva named Avalokiteshvara, who lived long ago.

The three major Buddhist sects are collectively referred to as the *Three Vehicles*, as *yana* is Sanskrit for "vehicle." The word Theravada means "School of the Elders," but it may be noted that Mahayana Buddhists have often referred to Theravada as *Hinayana*, which means "Lesser Vehicle." The word Mahayana means "Greater Vehicle." The word Vajrayana means "Diamond Vehicle."

Significant Times throughout the Year

Sacred times in Buddhism include, but are not limited to, the following:

Vesak: Also known as Buddha Day, this holiday commemorates the birth, enlightenment, and death of the Buddha.

Asalha Puja Day: Also known as Dharma Day, this day commemorates the Buddha's first sermon.

Magha Puja Day: Also known as Sangha Day, this day commemorates when 1,250 monks gathered at a temple to honor the Buddha.

New Year's Day: This day varies according to different Buddhist traditions.

Virtues in Buddhism

Anger Management

⁵Animosity does not eradicate animosity. Only by loving kindness is animosity dissolved. This law is ancient and eternal. (Dhammapada 1:5)

²Whoever controls his anger is like a true charioteer, in command of the rolling chariot and not just holding on the reins. (Dhammapada 17:2)

Forgiveness

⁶There are those who are aware that they are always facing death. Knowing this, they put aside all quarrels. (Dhammapada 1:6)

Gratitude

The Blessed One said, "Now what is the level of a person of no integrity? A person of no integrity is ungrateful and unthankful. This ingratitude, this lack of thankfulness, is advocated by rude people. It is

Buddhism

entirely on the level of people of no integrity. A person of integrity is grateful and thankful. This gratitude, this thankfulness, is advocated by civil people. It is entirely on the level of people of integrity." (Tripitaka: Sutta Pitaka: Anguttara Nikaya 2:32)

Humility

¹Shun anger, let go of pride, break out of every shackle. Whoever is not tied to possessions, clinging neither to body nor mind, is never in bondage. (Dhammapada 17:1)

Kindness

⁵To shun all evil. To do good. To purify one's heart. This is the teaching of the Buddhas. (Dhammapada 14:5)

¹⁵If one harms living beings, he cannot be considered noble. Only by exercising harmlessness toward living beings can one be called noble. (Dhammapada 19:15)

Love

Even as a mother would protect with her life her child, her only child, so too for all creatures unfold a boundless heart. With love for the whole world, unfold a boundless heart: above, below, all round, not constricted, without enemy or foe. (Tripitaka: Khuddaka Nikaya: Khuddakapatha 9)

Patience

[6]Patience that is enduring is the best discipline. Nirvana, says the Buddhas, is the highest goal. Whoever hurts another is not a monk. Whoever insults another is not a renunciate. (Dhammapada 14:6)

The Symbol of the Religion

The symbol that is often associated with Buddhism is the Dharma Wheel, called the *Dharmachakra* in Sanskrit, and it has eight spokes, representing the Eightfold Path. The rim symbolizes the completeness of the Buddha's teaching. In some depictions there are also three twirls in the center of the wheel, representing the Three Jewels of Buddhism: the Buddha, the Dharma, and the Sangha.

Chapter 4:
Christianity

Introduction

Christianity is the religion that was brought by Jesus (c. 4 B.C.E. – c. 30 C.E.) around the year 27 C.E. in the land of Judea, which was then under Roman occupation. A follower of Christianity is called a Christian, and there are approximately 2.38 billion Christians in the world. The scripture of Christianity is called the New Testament. Christians combine the New Testament with the Jewish Hebrew Bible, which Christians call the Old Testament, and they refer to the Old and New Testaments collectively as the (Christian) Bible. Some Christian Bibles also include a collection of works written in Greek with the Old Testament, and it is called the Apocrypha. The New Testament is also written in Greek. The place of worship for Christians is called a church.

A Christian spiritual leader of a congregation is called a pastor or a priest, depending on the sect.

Etymology

The key word in Christianity is "Christian," which means "follower of Christ." Christ is the anglicized version of *Christos*, which is the Greek word for Messiah, and it means "Anointed."

Purpose of Life

The purpose of human life in Christianity is to accept Jesus Christ as one's Lord and Savior, thereby having a right relationship with God. Through this, one's sins will be forgiven, and one will attain salvation from Hell and admittance into Heaven by God's grace. Christians also believe that they are to make disciples of Jesus among all nations for the glory of God.

Description of God

26Jesus looked at them and said, "With man this is impossible, but with God all things are possible." (New Testament: Matthew 19:26)

1In the beginning was the Word, and the Word was with God, and the Word was God. (New Testament: John 1:1)

16For God so loved the world that he gave his one and only Son, that whoever believes in him shall not perish but have eternal life. (New Testament: John 3:16)

21Whoever has my commands and keeps them is the one who loves me. The one who loves me will be loved by my Father, and I too will love them and show myself to them. (New Testament: John 14:21)

6Yet for us there is but one God, the Father, from whom all things came and for whom we live; and there is but one Lord, Jesus Christ, through whom all things came and through whom we live. (New Testament: 1 Corinthians 8:6)

6One God and Father of all, who is over all and through all and in all. (New Testament: Ephesians 4:6)

¹⁷He is before all things, and in him all things hold together. (New Testament: Colossians 1:17)

¹⁷Every good and perfect gift is from above, coming down from the Father of the heavenly lights, who does not change like shifting shadows. (New Testament: James 1:17)

¹⁹You believe that there is one God. Good! Even the demons believe that – and shudder. (New Testament: James 2:19)

²⁰If our hearts condemn us, we know that God is greater than our hearts, and he knows everything. (New Testament: 1 John 3:20)

¹⁶And so we know and rely on the love God has for us. God is love. Whoever lives in love lives in God, and God in them. (New Testament: 1 John 4:16)

⁵This is the message we have heard from him and declare to you: God is light; in him there is no darkness at all. (New Testament: 1 John 1:5)

⁸"I am the Alpha and the Omega," says the Lord God, "who is, and who was, and who is to come, the Almighty." (New Testament: Revelation 1:8)

[13]I am the Alpha and the Omega, the First and the Last, the Beginning and the End. (New Testament: Revelation 22:13)

These verses from the New Testament show that in Christianity God is understood to be One, Infinite, Loving, the Creator, the Sustainer, the All-Powerful, and the All-Knowing. God is often called Father in Christianity, and the Aramaic word for this is *Abba*, Aramaic being the language that Jesus spoke.

History and Description of the Religion

Christianity teaches that there exists one God, Who created everyone and everything, but there are three forms, or persons, of God: the Father, the Son, and the Holy Spirit. This doctrine is known as the *Trinity*, and while it is alluded to in the New Testament, it is elaborated on in different Christian creeds, notably the Nicene Creed. God the Father so loved the world that He sent His only begotten Son, Jesus Christ (who is God the Son), to die on a cross for the sins of humanity. The Holy Spirit is the third aspect of the Godhead, and

Christianity

He is known as the giver of life who has spoken through the prophets.

Jesus shared in the glory of God the Father before the creation of the world, and Christianity teaches that Jesus is the way, the truth, and the light, and through him all things were made. Christians believe that Jesus was born in human form in a Jewish setting to a righteous virgin named Mary, in Judea, around the year 4 B.C.E. Jesus grew up with a deep knowledge of Jewish scriptures, and when he was 30, he was baptized at his request by a man known as John the Baptist, who encouraged people to repent to God and who baptized people for the forgiveness of sins, which are wrongdoings. Jesus then began his ministry, traveling around the country and preaching the *Gospel*, or the "Good News," a message that salvation comes from devotion to God through belief in Jesus and that this faith results in love and service to others. He had the ability to perform miracles, which included the healing of the sick. Certain Jewish elites felt their power would be undermined by Jesus, so they turned him over to the Romans, and in Jerusalem the Roman governor Pontius Pilate

83

condemned Jesus to be crucified. Jesus died on the cross at the age of 33, and his body was put in a tomb, but he rose from the dead on the third day and ascended into Heaven to be at the right hand of the Father.

In the decades after the crucifixion, resurrection, and ascension of Jesus, his apostles and followers, notably a man named Paul, carried on his teachings and spread them to different regions, but there nevertheless arose different Christian sects and different Christian scriptures. Those who accepted the teachings of Paul are now known as Pauline Christians, and they were the predominant group, but there were also the Jewish Christians and the Gnostics. Christians remained a persecuted minority in the Roman Empire until the Roman emperor, Constantine, converted to Pauline Christianity, legalizing it in 313 C.E. with the Edict of Milan.

The Council of Nicaea was held in 325 C.E. to distinguish the dominant form of Christianity from Arian Christianity, which taught that Jesus had not always existed with God, that he was made by God the Father, and that he was subordinate to Him. Nicene Christianity teaches that Jesus is one with God the Father and the Holy Spirit. A standard Christian creed, known as the Nicene Creed, was developed by Christian Roman officials at this council. Christianity was made the official state religion of the Roman Empire in 380 C.E. with the Edict of Thessalonica, and the Nicene Creed was adjusted in the First Council of Constantinople in 381 C.E. Additional Roman councils would decide on which books were to be canonized into the Christian Bible, such as the Council of Rome in 382 C.E., the Council of Hippo in 393 C.E., and the Council of Carthage in 397 C.E. Arian Christianity would eventually die out.

In 431 C.E., the Council of Ephesus was held to distinguish the majority of Nicene Christians, who believed that Jesus is fully man and fully God, from those who believed that Jesus is two persons in one body – one human person and one Divine person. Because of this distinction, the latter group did not refer to Mary as "the mother of God," but rather as "the mother of Christ." This group became known as the Church of the East, and it was centered around the teachings of a man named

Nestorius, so it is sometimes called Nestorian Christianity. It is today represented by the Assyrian Church of the East.

In 451 C.E., the Council of Chalcedon lead to the distinction between Chalcedonian Christianity, which is the majority, and Oriental Orthodox Christianity, which is also known as Miaphysitism. There are a few Oriental Orthodox churches, and they believe that Jesus is one person with one nature, which is both Divine and human. In contrast, Chalcedonian churches believe that Jesus is one person with two natures – one Divine and one human. The largest Oriental Orthodox church is currently the Ethiopian Orthodox Tewahedo Church. Note that the word Miaphysitism is sometimes used interchangeably with the word Monophysitism.

In 1054, the Great Schism occurred between the Roman Catholic Church in the West and the Eastern Orthodox Church in the East (which is different from the Oriental Orthodox Church). Until then, the Roman Catholic and Eastern Orthodox churches had been united as one church. Over time, cultural and political differences caused tensions between the two and led to disagreements, although there came to be some doctrinal differences as well. For example, the Nicene Creed mentions the Holy Spirit, and both churches accept this. However, the Eastern Orthodox Church believes that the creed should say that the Holy Spirit proceeds from the Father, whereas the Roman Catholic Church added that the Holy Spirit proceeds from the Father and the Son. This particular line of the Nicene Creed is known as the Filioque Clause. The Eastern Orthodox Church also rejects the supreme worldly authority of the Pope, who is the leader of the Roman Catholic Church. They believed that the Pope was simply the Bishop (i.e., congregational leader) of Rome, who was the first among equals. The *clergy*, or spiritual leadership, also differs between Catholicism and Eastern Orthodoxy. The Catholic hierarchy of the clergy from least to greatest consists of deacons, priests, bishops, archbishops, cardinals, and the Pope. The Eastern Orthodox hierarchy of the clergy from least to greatest consists of readers, subdeacons, deacons, priests, and bishops.

A Comparison of Six Major World Religions

In 1517, a German Catholic priest named Martin Luther published 95 theses in protest against the Roman Catholic Church. Luther argued that the Christian Bible, not the Pope, should serve as the religious authority in this world. Luther also argued that salvation was only by the grace of God and that people could do nothing to earn their salvation. This was the beginning of the Protestant Reformation, and Luther was not the only reformer. Around the same time, the King of England, Henry VIII, broke away from the Catholic Church to form the Anglican Church because the Pope would not grant him a divorce. Figures including Huldrych Zwingli, William Farel, and Jean Calvin led a reformation away from the Catholic Church in Switzerland, and John Knox led reformers in Scotland. The recent invention of the printing press greatly aided the Protestant Reformation because the Bible was now being printed in different languages and made available to anyone who could read. These movements led to the creation of the Lutheran, Anglican, and Calvinist (or "Reformed") denominations of Protestantism. Over the next few centuries those denominations would splinter into more denominations such as the Presbyterians, Anabaptists, Quakers, Baptists, Methodists, and more.

New movements would eventually form in North America during the 19th and 20th centuries, including the Restorationists, which led to the Churches of Christ; the Church of Jesus Christ of Latter-day Saints, also referred to as Mormonism; the Adventists, or Millerites, which led to the Seventh-day Adventist Church, the Advent Christian Church, and the Church of God; the Jehovah's Witnesses; and the Pentecostals.

Christians believe that the Old Testament is filled with prophecies about Jesus, and they believe that he is the Messiah that the Jews await. The New Testament teaches that the sacred Jewish book called the Torah, often translated as "the Law," was sent to expose the sinful nature of humanity as humans fell short of keeping it, but the sacrifice of Jesus on the cross fulfilled the Law, thereby doing away with its works and their necessity, but not doing away with its moral teachings, such as loving God and loving others. Consequently, many Christians view the numerous laws of the Old Testament that are not repeated in the New Testament as not applicable, although some Christians keep them. However, it should be noted that Christians view the Ten Commandments as rules of morality that one should try to keep. Additionally, Christians generally number the Ten Commandments slightly differently than the Jews, although the wording is the same.

Humanity is inherently sinful, meaning that humans are inherently inclined to do wrong. Humans inherited this sinful nature from Adam and Eve, who committed the original sin of eating from the forbidden tree in the Garden of Eden. Sin makes humanity destined for Hell, a place of fire and torture experienced after death. There exist spiritual beings called angels, and they serve God. However, unlike in Judaism, Christians believe that angels can disobey God. An angel named Lucifer, who would come to be known as Satan, or the Devil, rebelled against God, so God cast him, and the angels who followed him, out of Heaven. Christians refer to fallen angels as demons, and after having become a fallen angel, Satan further tempts people to do evil, making the path to Hell appear alluring. One is saved from Hell by accepting Jesus Christ as their Lord and Savior, believing that he took on the sins of humanity when he died on the cross, and consequently his followers are absolved of their sins by the grace of God. If one is a sincere follower of Jesus, it is expected that they will naturally incline to do good deeds, which are the works of the Spirit, but they are still encouraged to avoid bad deeds, which are the works of the flesh.

Christians believe that there will be a second coming of Jesus. He will return to Earth from Heaven and then rule the Earth in an era of peace and justice for 1,000 years. All those of humanity that have died will be physically resurrected, and Jesus will judge everyone based on their acceptance of him. Those who did not accept Jesus as their Lord and Savior will be cast into Hell. Certain Christians interpret the New Testament as teaching that those in Hell will remain in it forever, whereas other Christians interpret the New Testament as teaching that those in Hell will be annihilated in body and soul, ceasing to exist. Those who accepted Jesus as their Lord and Savior will live in Heaven, a place of bliss and reward.

Recall the different Christian sects mentioned earlier, which include Catholicism, Protestantism, Eastern Orthodoxy, Oriental Orthodoxy, and the Church of the East. As stated earlier, within each sect there can be different denominations. Certain Christian sects have different rituals called sacraments through which they reach out to God, and many Christians, including those of certain Protestant denominations, recognize at least two: baptism and the eucharist, the latter of which is also known as communion or the Lord's supper. And even with these two sacraments, Christians differ as to how exactly they perform them.

When someone is baptized, they are either immersed in a body of water or have water poured on their head, depending on the sect or denomination, and the ritual is performed in the name of the Father, the Son, and the Holy Spirit.

The eucharist involves consuming a piece of bread that is the body of Christ and sipping some wine (or grape juice) that is the blood of

Christ. Some Christians believe this ritual is symbolic, but others believe that the bread and the wine take on the actual properties of the body and blood of Christ. Through the eucharist, one reaffirms their commitment to Christ and receives strength from him. There are also other sacraments accepted by certain sects, and these sacraments include confirmation, penance, marriage, holy orders, and anointing of the sick. Note that all Christians believe in the concept of marriage but not necessarily as a sacrament. Also note that most Christians typically gather to worship in churches on Sunday because that is the day on which Jesus was resurrected from the dead.

Significant Times throughout the Year

Sacred times in Christianity include, but are not limited to, the following:

Christmas: This day commemorates the birth of Jesus.

Lent: This is a forty-day period before Easter in which certain Christians self-reflect and fast, often giving up something pleasurable.

Easter: This day commemorates the resurrection of Jesus from the dead.

Pentecost: This day commemorates the coming of the Holy Spirit to Jesus's apostles, who were his close companions, after Jesus ascended into Heaven. It takes place 50 days after Easter.

All Saints' Day: On this day, Catholics, Orthodox Christians, and some Protestants revere Christian saints.

Virtues in Christianity

Anger Management

[19]*My dear brothers and sisters, take note of this: Everyone should be quick to listen, slow to speak and slow to become angry,* [20]*because human anger does not*

produce the righteousness that God desires. (New Testament: James 1:19-20)

Forgiveness

[14]For if you forgive other people when they sin against you, your heavenly Father will also forgive you. (New Testament: Matthew 6:14)

[33]When they came to the place called the Skull, they crucified him there, along with the criminals—one on his right, the other on his left. [34]Jesus said, "Father, forgive them, for they do not know what they are doing." And they divided up his clothes by casting lots. (New Testament: Luke 23:33-34)

Gratitude

[30]When he was at the table with them, he took bread, gave thanks, broke it and began to give it to them. (New Testament: Luke 24:30)

[18]Give thanks in all circumstances; for this is God's will for you in Christ Jesus. (New Testament: 1 Thessalonians 5:18)

Humility

[11]For all those who exalt themselves will be humbled, and those who humble themselves will be exalted. (New Testament: Luke 14:11)

Kindness

[31]Do to others as you would have them do to you. (New Testament: Luke 6:31)

[36]Be merciful, just as your Father is merciful. (New Testament: Luke 6:36)

[22]But the fruit of the Spirit is love, joy, peace, forbearance, kindness, goodness, faithfulness, [23]gentleness and self-control. Against such things there is no law. (New Testament: Galatians 5:22-23)

Love

[34]A new command I give you: Love one another. As I have loved you, so you must love one another. (New Testament: John 13:34)

⁷Dear friends, let us love one another, for love comes from God. Everyone who loves has been born of God and knows God. ⁸Whoever does not love does not know God, because God is love. (New Testament: 1 John 4:7-8)

Patience

²Be completely humble and gentle; be patient, bearing with one another in love. (New Testament: Ephesians 4:2)

The Symbol of the Religion

The symbol that is often associated with Christianity is the cross. It represents the cross that Jesus was crucified on as an atonement for the sins of humanity.

Chapter 5: Islam

Introduction

Islam is the religion that was brought by Muhammad (c. 570 – 632 C.E.) around the year 610 C.E. in the city of Mecca, in the Hijaz region of Arabia (modern-day Saudi Arabia). A follower of Islam is called a Muslim, and there are approximately 1.91 billion Muslims in the world. It should be noted that Muslims view Islam as a revival of the religion of Abraham and the prophets before and after him. The scripture of Islam is called the Qur'an (sometimes spelled "Koran"). The other source of Islam is called the Sunnah, which is the example of Muhammad based on his sayings, actions, and approvals. The Sunnah is recorded in books that contain narrations called hadiths, and it is widely accepted that the top two authentic hadith books are Sahih Al-Bukhari and Sahih Muslim. The Qur'an and the hadiths are written in Arabic. The place of worship for

Muslims is called a mosque (in Arabic: *masjid*). A Muslim spiritual leader of a congregation is called an imam. The title "imam" can also refer to a scholar or a prayer leader.

Etymology

The word "Islam" is derived from the Arabic trilateral root S-L-M (*salima*). Salima means to be safe from defects, and Islam means "Submission (to the will of God)." The word "Islam" is etymologically related to the Arabic word *salam*, which means "peace." A "Muslim" is, consequently, one who peacefully submits to the will of God (i.e., one who adheres to the religion of Islam).

Purpose of Life

The purpose of human life in Islam is to serve God through correct belief and good deeds. The Qur'an also enjoins Muslims to encourage others to truth and patience. After the end of the world, all of creation will be resurrected and given life by God, and there will be a Day of Judgment. If one had faith and their good deeds outweigh their bad deeds on the Day of Judgment, then God will have mercy on them, and they will be admitted into Paradise, also known as Heaven, the Garden, and *Jannah* in Arabic. If one did not have faith or their bad deeds outweigh their good deeds on the Day of Judgment, then they will be sent to Hell (in Arabic: *Jahannam*), also known as the Fire, *An-Nar*.

Description of God

All praise is for God, the Lord of all worlds, [2]the Infinitely Good, the Most Merciful, [3]Master of the Day of Judgment. [4]You alone do we worship, and You alone do we ask for help. [5]Guide us on the Straight Path, [6]the path of those You are gracious to; [7]not of those You are angry with; nor of those who go astray. (Qur'an 1)

[255]God, there is no god but He, the Ever-Living, the Self-Subsisting. Neither drowsiness nor sleep overtakes Him. To Him belongs whatever is in the heavens and whatever is on the earth. Who is it that could intercede with Him except by His permission? He knows what is before them and what is behind them, and they do not

comprehend anything of His knowledge except what He
pleases. His Seat encompasses the heavens and the
earth, and it does not tire Him to preserve them both,
for He is the Most High, the Absolute Greatest.
(Qur'an 2:255)

*102*That is God – your Lord! There is no god but He,
the Creator of everything; so worship Him, for He
maintains everything. (Qur'an 6:102)

*35*God is the Light of the heavens and the earth. His
light is as a niche in which there is a lamp, and the
lamp is in a glass. The glass is as though it were a
glittering star. It is lit from a blessed olive tree, neither
of the east nor of the west, the oil of which would nearly
give light though no fire touched it – light upon light!
God guides to His light whom He pleases; and God
strikes out parables for men, and God knows all things.
(Qur'an 24:35)

*1*Whatever is in the heavens and the earth glorifies God,
for He is the Almighty, the Most Wise. *2*His is the
kingdom of the heavens and the earth. He gives life, and
He causes death, and He has power over everything. *3*He
is the First and the Last; and the Outer and the Inner;
and He has knowledge of everything. (Qur'an 57:1-3)

[14] And He is the Most Forgiving, the Most Loving, [15] the Lord of the Glorious Throne; [16] the Doer of whatever He will. (Qur'an 85:14-16)

[1] Say, 'He is God, the One, [2] God the Eternal, on Whom all depend. [3] He has never had offspring, and He was not born. [4] And no one is comparable to Him.' (Qur'an 112)

Abu Musa narrated: The Messenger of God was standing among us, and he said five things, "Indeed, God, Mighty and Sublime, does not sleep, and it does not befit Him to sleep. He lowers the scale (of justice), and He lifts it. The deeds of the night ascend to Him before the deeds of the day, and the deeds of the day before the night. His veil is light. If He were to uncover Himself, the splendor of His countenance would incinerate His creation as far as His sight reaches. (Sahih Muslim, Hadith 179)

These verses from the Qur'an, and this hadith, show that in Islam God is understood to be One, Infinite, Loving, Light, the Creator, the Sustainer, the All-Powerful, and the All-Knowing. In Islam, God is often referred to with the Arabic name *Allah*, or with the title *Rabb*, which means "Lord."

It should perhaps be noted that in the Qur'an, God often refers to Himself alone in the plural (We, Us, Our, etc.). This concept is known as the "royal we," and it is used by figures of authority to refer to themselves alone. God often uses this literary technique while referring to Himself alone.

History and Description of the Religion

Thousands of years ago, a significant prophet named Abraham had two sons: Ishmael and Isaac. Isaac settled in Canaan, and his descendants included the Israelites, among them Moses and Jesus. Ishmael settled in a place in Arabia that would eventually be called Mecca (also spelled: "Makkah"). Abraham and Ishmael built the first house of worship to God there, called the *Ka'bah* (also spelled: "Kaaba"), and the Ka'bah is part of Al-Masjid Al-Haram, the most sacred mosque in Islam. However, the descendants of Ishmael eventually turned to polytheism, idolatry, warfare, and vices.

Thousands of years later, there existed a descendant of Abraham through Ishmael named Muhammad, who was from the ruling tribe of Quraysh in Mecca. Born around 570 C.E. and orphaned from a young age, Muhammad grew to have a strong reputation for truthfulness, generosity, and monotheism. He was a merchant, and he married and had children. Muhammad started receiving revelations from God through the Angel Gabriel at the age of 40, and these revelations were called the *Qur'an*, which means the "Recitation." The first revelation came after the Angel Gabriel embraced Muhammad while Muhammad was in a cave called Hira in the Mountain of Light, or *Jabal An-Nur*.

After an initial period of private preaching, Muhammad began publicly preaching the message of Islam, calling his people to peaceful, kind, and charitable ways, and while many accepted it, most of the Quraysh were strongly opposed to it because it promoted monotheism. God also performed miracles through Muhammad such as several accurate prophecies, an instance in which the moon split and came back together, and, later in his life, an instance where he produced water from his fingers, supplying a multitude of people with water.

However, the Qur'an was, and still is, regarded as the greatest miracle due to its unequalled divine language.

Over the years, the Quraysh ridiculed, boycotted, and tortured the Muslims in Mecca, at times going so far as to even kill. This was only due to the monotheism of the Muslims, which the Quraysh resented, but Muhammad and the Muslims patiently endured the oppression.

On one night, the Prophet experienced an event that would come to be known as the Night Journey and the Ascension, or *Al-Isra' wal-Mi'raj*. The Angel Gabriel woke Muhammad, and the latter was transported by a white winged horse-like creature, called Al-Buraq, larger than a donkey but smaller than a mule. It took Muhammad to Jerusalem, and there he led previous prophets of God in prayer. This occurred at a place known as Al-Masjid Al-Aqsa, which is the third most sacred mosque in Islam, and it is in the same area where the Jews believe their Temple used to be. It should be noted that Muslims believe that Al-Masjid Al-Aqsa was the second mosque to be built in the history of humanity, implying that it was built before Solomon. Muslims also believe that Solomon rebuilt the mosque. However, during the time of Muhammad, the land where the mosque had been was barren, and the building was rebuilt after the Prophet's time. That same night, from Al-Masjid Al-Aqsa, Muhammad also ascended into Heaven, where he met the Prophets Adam, Jesus Christ, John (the Baptist), Joseph, Idris, Aaron, Moses, and Abraham, before he was brought to the presence of God, and God enjoined on him and his followers the daily formal prayers. Thereafter Muhammad descended back and returned to Mecca that night.

Eventually, people in a city to the north accepted Islam, and most of the Muslims migrated there. Muhammad migrated there in the year 622 C.E., and this event is called the *Hijrah*, and it marks the start of the Islamic lunar calendar, called the *Hijri* calendar. The city to which the Muslims migrated would become known as Medina (also spelled: "Al-Madinah"). Many Jews lived there too, and the Muslims made alliances with them. In Medina, the Muslims built Al-Masjid An-Nabawi, the second most sacred mosque in Islam, and the house of the Prophet Muhammad was connected to it.

The belligerence of the Quraysh persisted, and the Muslims fought them in a few battles to maintain the security of the Muslim community in Medina. Additionally, the Jewish tribes in Medina broke their treaties with the Muslims and took up arms against them because they disliked the religious and political influence of the new Muslim community, even though the Prophet Muhammad had not provoked them. In three separate incidents, the Muslims were victorious over the Jewish tribes. It should be noted that, in accordance with the Qur'an and the Sunnah, Muslims are not allowed to force people to convert to Islam (see: Qur'an 2:256), and war is only allowed out of defense, justice, and security (see: Qur'an 2:190-195, 22:39-40, 4:75). Moreover, the word *jihad* means "struggle," and it can refer to various forms of outer or inner struggles.

Eventually, the Muslims were also victorious over the Quraysh, and the tribe converted to Islam, with the Ka'bah being rededicated to God alone. Other battles were fought against communities that mobilized against the Muslims, and the Muslims often continued to be victorious. All of this time Islam had been spreading, and the number of Muslims in Arabia had increased into a nation, or an *ummah*. Muhammad led the Muslims in the Hajj pilgrimage to Mecca and soon afterward passed away in Medina at the age of 63, in the year 632 C.E. His age was determined by the Islamic lunar calendar, which differs from the Gregorian calendar. In accordance with a command in the Qur'an, Muslims say *sallallahu 'alayhi wa sallam*, which means "commendations and peace from God be upon him" whenever they mention the Prophet Muhammad's name, but they do not worship or deify him.

After the death of the Prophet Muhammad, the ruler of the Muslim community was called a *caliph*, and the first four caliphs were his closest companions, who ruled one after another: Abu Bakr, 'Umar, 'Uthman, and 'Ali. These four are collectively known as the *Rightly Guided Caliphs*, and their government is known as the *Rashidun Caliphate*, which lasted from 632 to 661 C.E. During this era, wars were fought between the Muslims and other communities and nations.

These wars led to the Muslim conquest of the Persian Sassanid Empire and the Middle Eastern territories of the Eastern Roman Empire as well as certain North African territories. The Rashidun Caliphate also oversaw the preservation of the Qur'an. During the time of Abu Bakr, the Qur'an was written down into one volume, and during the time of 'Uthman, copies of it were made and distributed. Also, during the time of 'Umar, Al-Masjid Al-Aqsa was rebuilt in Jerusalem. Eventually, misunderstandings among rulers, as well as the manipulations of power hungry people, led to civil war within the Muslim world, and the Rashidun Caliphate ended.

Thereafter, the Muslim world was ruled by the Umayyad Dynasty from 661 to 750 C.E. After the Umayyads, much of the Muslim world was ruled by the 'Abbasid Dynasty, which lasted from 750 to 1258 C.E. During these two dynasties, religious schools of thought, or *madhhabs*, formed. They were centered around the teachings of jurisprudence of different renowned scholars. Note that jurisprudence is the science of law, and in Arabic it is called *fiqh*. The law itself, which includes all the rulings from the Qur'an and the Sunnah, is called *Sharia*.

Additionally, schools of *'aqidah*, or "creed," formed, and they differed regarding certain matters of belief. Very knowledgeable scholars also compiled *hadith* books, detailing the sayings, actions, and approvals of the Prophet Muhammad. These works laid the foundation for future seekers of knowledge. Although the canonical hadith books were compiled around the 9th century C.E., which was approximately two centuries after the Prophet Muhammad, hadiths had actually been collected since the time of his companions in the 7th century C.E. Moreover, there is a complex methodology used in discerning a hadith's authenticity, and it involves analyzing a hadith's *matn* (text) and *isnad* (chain of narrators between the hadith collector and the Prophet). Note that in English translations of hadiths, the isnad is often not translated in order to maintain brevity. It may additionally be noted that biographical narratives about the Prophet Muhammad are recorded in a genre of literature known as *seerah* (also spelled: "sirah").

As with other religions, there are different sects in Islam, and the two largest are the Sunni and the Shia, although the overwhelming majority of the Muslim world is Sunni. Sunnis and Shias differ politically and legally, but not theologically. The difference between the two started when certain Muslims believed that 'Ali, the Prophet's cousin, should have succeeded him in leadership and that the role of leader was rightfully passed down through 'Ali's descendants. These are the Shia Muslims. Sunni Muslims accept the four caliphs mentioned earlier as rightful leaders. Although there is only one Qur'an, Sunnis have six main hadith books, whereas Shias have four main hadith books. The two most authentic, or *sahih*, Sunni hadith books were compiled by Muhammad ibn Isma'il Al-Bukhari (810 – 870 C.E.) and Muslim ibn Al-Hajjaj (820 – 875 C.E.), so these two books are called *Sahih Al-Bukhari* and *Sahih Muslim*.

In Islam, there is a very significant hadith called the *Gabriel Hadith* (in Arabic: *Hadith Jibreel*). In it, the Angel Gabriel reviewed the *deen*, or religion, with the Prophet Muhammad in front of some of the Prophet's companions. According to the Gabriel Hadith, there are three fundamental aspects of the religion: Islam, Iman, and Ihsan.

Significant Islamic ritual practices are often summarized in the form of the 5 Pillars of Islam:

Shahadah: To bear witness: "I testify that there is no god except Allah, and I testify that Muhammad is the Messenger of Allah" (in Arabic: "*Ash-hadu an la ilaha illallah, wa ash-hadu anna Muhammadar-rasulullah*").

Salah: To perform 5 daily formal prayers. The prayers are *Fajr* (during dawn), *Zuhr* (during the early afternoon), *'Asr* (during the late afternoon), *Maghrib* (during sunset), and *'Isha* (during the early night). Friday is holiest day of the week in Islam, in part because Adam, the first man, was created on that day. On Fridays, Zuhr is replaced by *Jumu'ah*, when Muslims gather at the mosque to listen to the imam give a sermon and then perform a congregational prayer. Muslims perform salah while facing the Ka'bah in Mecca, but they do not pray *to* the Ka'bah; they pray to God. The Ka'bah may be thought of as a rallying point, but it is not the focus of worship.

Zakah: To give in charity 2.5% of one's savings (and a certain portion of one's livestock, merchandise, and harvest, if applicable), provided they reach a certain amount after one lunar year. Zakah is different from regular charity, which is called *sadaqah*.

Sawm: To fast (abstaining from water, food, sexual activity, and anything else that breaks the fast) every day, from dawn to sunset, during the lunar month of Ramadan. Ramadan is holy because it is the month in which the Qur'an was first revealed. Another word for Sawm is Siyam.

Hajj: To perform a pilgrimage to certain sites in Mecca and surrounding areas at least once in one's life if one is able to. Hajj can only be performed during a certain time of the year. There is also a minor pilgrimage to Mecca called 'Umrah. It has fewer rituals, it is not obligatory, and it can be performed throughout the year, but Hajj is the one that is obligatory.

Islam belongs to a group of faiths known as the "Abrahamic Religions" (usually known to be Judaism, Christianity, and Islam), as they all have ties to a Semitic prophet named Abraham who lived a few thousand years ago. As such, Muslims share many of the same beliefs held by Jews and

Christians. According to the Gabriel Hadith, Islamic beliefs are usually summarized in the 6 Pillars of Iman (Faith):

1. Belief in God (in Arabic: Allah)

Allah is the Arabic name for the one God, and even Arab Jews and Arab Christians refer to God as Allah. For an outline of some of the qualities of God, see the section "Description of God." Also note that the One that Christians call "the Father" is the same One that Muslims call "God," but Muslims believe that God prefers that humanity does not refer to Him as a Father. Instead of the wording of "the Father and His children," Muslims believe in the wording of "the Creator and His creations."

2. Belief in God's Angels

Angels are beings of light that carry out orders from God and worship Him. They do not disobey God, so there is no concept in Islam of "fallen angels." Islam teaches that every person has two guardian angels and two angels that record one's good deeds and bad deeds. Three particularly important angels in Islam are Gabriel, the angel in charge of revelation; Michael, the angel in charge of rain and plants; and Israfil, the angel in charge of blowing the horn that will signal the Last Day. Muslims believe that Gabriel is the Holy Spirit, and Islam rejects the notion of the Trinity, so Gabriel is viewed as distinct from God. Moreover, angels are different from jinns, which are unseen beings in this world with free will. In Islam, Satan, whose name is Iblis, is a jinn, not an angel, and he arrogantly chose the path of evil. God allows Satan to tempt people to do evil in order to test whether they will choose good. Also note that the word jinn may be spelled "djinn," and the singular of the word can also be the plural.

3. **Belief in God's Books**

Books of God are scriptures that were revealed by Him through prophets to inform, guide, and warn humanity. The final book from God is the Qur'an, which confirms that the Torah and the Gospel were also from God. However, Muslims believe that the Torah and the Gospel were altered by people, whereas the Qur'an is, and will remain, unaltered. Consequently, Muslims neither affirm nor disaffirm certain stories and laws that are in the Bible but not addressed in Islam, as long as they do not contradict Islam. If the Qur'an and the authentic hadiths approve something, Muslims approve it; if the Qur'an and the authentic hadiths reject something, Muslims reject it; and if the Qur'an and the authentic hadiths neither approve nor reject something, Muslims leave it alone.

4. **Belief in God's Messengers**

A "prophet" was one who received some sort of clear revelation from

God and had to convey it. Among the prophets were men known as "messengers," and these were prophets who were sent to disbelieving peoples. Therefore, every messenger was a prophet, but not every prophet was a messenger. Five of the most significant messengers were Noah, Abraham, Moses, Jesus, and Muhammad. Islam teaches that Muhammad was the final prophet and messenger, and there will be no new prophet or messenger after him. It should also be noted that Muslims love and revere Jesus and believe that he was the Christ/Messiah, born to the Virgin Mary, but Islam teaches that he was not God or the Son of God; Jesus was fully human. The Qur'an also teaches that Jesus was not crucified, and a hadith states that it was one of Jesus's disciples, who was made to look like him, who was crucified. God allowed Jesus to ascend to Heaven without having died, and he will return to Earth from Heaven in the last days and be a Muslim leader. In Islam, instead of a crucifixion, it is God's mercy that leads to salvation from Hellfire.

5. Belief in the Last Day

The Last Day is also known as the Day of Judgement, the Day of Resurrection, and other names. It is the Day on which humans, jinns, and all of God's creations will perish. Then the world will be recreated, and everyone will be physically resurrected. On that Day, humans and jinns will be judged by God based on their faith and their deeds, and thereafter each individual will be sent either to Hell or to Paradise. Paradise lasts for eternity. Many Muslims interpret the Qur'an as stating that Hell will also last for eternity. However, some individuals who had proper faith but lacked good deeds will eventually be taken out of Hell, rejuvenated, and then placed in Paradise for eternity.

Islam

6. Belief in God's Decree

The Decree is the notion that God has
already decreed everything, good and
bad, in the past, present, and future.
According to Muslims, this does not
contradict the notion of humans and
jinns having free will. God, being the
All-Knowing, already knew what
people's choices and actions in their
lives would be, and He recorded them
all and ordained them. Therefore,
God's Decree may be thought of as
God's Foreknowledge. Humans and
jinns must still strive to do good deeds
that are within their capacity.

The word *Ihsan* means "Excellence," and in
practice it means to worship God as if you see
Him, for even though you do not see Him, He
sees you.

Islam also forbids many actions that the
religion labels as sinful, including: idolatry,
murdering innocents, disrespecting one's

119

parents, theft, adultery, fornication, bearing false witness, consuming intoxicants, gambling, magic, slander, dealing with interest payments, and consuming forbidden meat such as pork. Note also that the word *halal* means "permissible" or "lawful," and the word *haram* means "impermissible" or "unlawful."

Significant Times throughout the Year

Besides every Jumu'ah and Ramadan, there are other sacred times throughout the year in Islam, and they include the following:

Yawm 'Ashura: This is the day on which God saved Moses and his people from Pharaoh, and fasting on this day can lead to the forgiveness of minor sins from the previous year. Yawm 'Ashura is on the 10th of the Islamic month of Muharram. This is also the day on which the grandson of the Prophet Muhammad, Al-Husayn, was martyred, so Shia Muslims mourn on this day.

Laylatul-Qadr (the Night of Power): It is the night on which the Qur'an was first revealed, it is worth more than one thousand months, and praying during it can lead to the forgiveness of one's minor sins.

Eid Al-Fitr: This is the first day after Ramadan, and it is a celebratory day, marking the end of the fast.

Yawm 'Arafah: This is the day on which the religion was completed, and fasting on this day can lead to the forgiveness of two years of minor sins.

Eid Al-Adha: This is a celebratory day during the time of Hajj. It is the day after Yawm 'Arafah, and Muslims around the world slaughter livestock animals and distribute the meat to the poor.

Virtues in Islam

Anger Management

Abu Hurayrah narrated: The Messenger of God said, "The strong man is not the good wrestler, but the strong man is one who controls himself when angry." (Sahih

Al-Bukhari, Hadith 6114; Sahih Muslim, Hadith 2609; Riyad As-Salihin, Hadith 45)

Abu Hurayrah narrated: A man said to the Prophet, "Advise me." The Prophet said, "Do not become angry." The man repeated his request several times, and the Prophet replied, "Do not become angry." (Sahih Al-Bukhari, Hadith 6116; Riyad As-Salihin, Hadith 48)

Forgiveness

[22] *And do not let those amongst you who have plenty and ample means swear that they will not give anything to their relatives and the poor and those who have emigrated in God's cause, but let them pardon and overlook. Do you not like God to forgive you? And God is Most Forgiving, Most Merciful. (Qur'an 24:22)*

[14] *Say to those who believe that they forgive those who hope not for God's days, so that He may reward people for that which they have earned. (Qur'an 45:14)*

'Abdullah ibn Mas'ud narrated: It is as if I can see the Messenger of God tell the story of a prophet who had been beaten by his people, who was wiping the blood from his face, and who was saying, "My Lord, forgive

my people, for they do not know." (Sahih Al-Bukhari, Hadith 6929; Riyad As-Salihin, Hadith 645)

Gratitude

[145]No soul can die except by God's permission at a destined time. And anyone who wishes for the reward of this world, We will give him some of it; and anyone who wishes for the reward of the Hereafter, We will give him some of it. And We will reward the grateful. (Qur'an 3:145)

[7]When your Lord proclaimed, 'If you give thanks, I will certainly give you more; but if you are ungrateful, My torment is truly severe!' (Qur'an 14:7)

Humility

[63]And the servants of the Infinitely Good are those who walk on the earth humbly, and when the ignorant address them, they say, 'Peace!' (Qur'an 25:63)

Kindness

[36]And worship God, and do not associate anything with Him; and show kindness to your parents, and to

relatives, orphans, the poor, the neighbor who is near, the neighbor who is far, close friends, travelers in need, and bondspeople in your possession. Indeed, God does not like whoever is arrogant and boastful. (Qur'an 4:36)

[34]Good and evil are not equal. Repel evil with what is best. Then you will see that one who was once your enemy has become like a close friend. (Qur'an 41:34)

Jarir ibn 'Abdullah narrated: The Messenger of God said, "God will not be merciful to whoever is not merciful to mankind." (Sahih Al-Bukhari, Hadith 7376; Riyad As-Salihin, Hadith 227)

'Abdullah ibn 'Amr ibn Al-'As narrated: The Messenger of God said, "He who wants to be saved from the Fire and enter the Garden should die believing in God and the Last Day and should do to others what he wishes to be done to him." (Sahih Muslim, Hadith 1844; Riyad As-Salihin, Hadith 1566)

'A'ishah narrated: The Prophet said, "Indeed, God is Gentle and loves gentleness in all matters." (Sahih Al-Bukhari, Hadith 6927; Riyad As-Salihin, Hadith 632)

Love

*Abu Hurayrah narrated: The Messenger of God said,
"You will not enter Paradise until you believe, and you
will not believe until you love one another. Should I not
direct you to a thing which, if you do it, you will love
one another? Give (the greeting of) peace amongst you."
(Sahih Muslim, Hadith 54; Riyad As-Salihin,
Hadith 378)*

Patience

[45]*Seek help with patience and prayer, though it is indeed
a difficult thing except for the humble. (Qur'an 2:45)*

[200]*O you who believe, be patient, compete in being
patient, be on guard, and fear God, so that you may be
successful. (Qur'an 3:200)*

The Symbol of the Religion

The symbol that is often associated with
Islam is the crescent moon and the star.
However, this is not actually something that is
prescribed in Islam. It originated from the
Turks during World War II as a symbol for
Islamic relief efforts just as the red cross was a

symbol for Christian relief efforts. The symbol became culturally tied to Islam. A significance of the moon in Islam is that the religion goes by a lunar calendar, but neither the Prophet Muhammad nor his companions ever designated this to be the symbol of Islam. Moreover, there is no official symbol that the religion of Islam designated for itself.

Chapter 6: Sikhism

Introduction

Sikhism is the religion that was brought by Nanak (1469 – 1539 C.E.) around the year 1497 C.E. near Sultanpur in India. The religion was perpetuated by nine successors after Nanak and formalized by Gobind Singh (1666 – 1708 C.E.) in 1699 C.E. A follower of Sikhism is called a Sikh, and many Sikhs refer to Sikhism as *Sikhi*, so the term Sikhi will be used in this book. There are approximately 25 million Sikhs in the world. The main scripture of Sikhi is the Guru Granth Sahib, and another significant scripture is the Dasam Granth. They are written in many different languages, mainly using a script called Gurmukhi. The place of worship for Sikhs is called a Gurdwara. There is no clergy in Sikhi, but the one who oversees a gurdwara, counsels a *sangat* (congregation), and reads from the Guru Granth Sahib during worship services is called a granthi.

Etymology

The work "Sikh" is actually pronounced closer to "sick" as opposed to "seek." "Sikh" means a "learner" or "disciple," as the Punjabi verb *sikhna* means "to learn." Sikhs are disciples of the Guru.

The word "guru," originally a Sanskrit word, means "the light that dispels all darkness," and it is often used in Hinduism to refer to a spiritual teacher. In Sikhi, God is the ultimate guru, but there were also ten human gurus, beginning with Nanak and ending with Gobind Singh. These gurus are regarded as more than regular spiritual teachers, and they are said to be the embodiment of God's divine light, in union with Him. After the death of Guru Gobind Singh, the status of guru passed to the Sikh holy book, the Adi Granth, so it is now known as the Guru Granth Sahib.

Purpose of Life

The purpose of human life in Sikhi is to live normally, performing duties that include work and marriage, while remembering God, the

Divine, and performing *seva*, or selfless service. Remembrance of the Divine is called *simran*, and it is accomplished through recitation of the sacred songs from the Guru Granth Sahib. Seva is accomplished through earnest, honest work and sharing with others. Through these practices, a Sikh loses fear of death and rebirth and lives according to *Hukam*, the Divine Command. Ultimately, Sikhs hope to attain *mukti*, or "liberation." Mukti refers to when a soul merges with God, thereby transcending the cycle of reincarnation.

Description of God

One Universal Creator God. The Name Is Truth. Creative Being Personified. No Fear. No Hatred. Image Of The Undying, Beyond Birth, Self-Existent. By Guru's Grace. (Guru Granth Sahib, Page 1)

Amongst all is the Light – You [i.e., God] are that Light. By this Illumination, that Light is radiant within all. Through the Guru's Teachings, the Light shines forth. (Guru Granth Sahib, Page 13)

God is All-powerful, Vast, Lofty and Infinite. (Guru Granth Sahib, Page 107)

The Lord is kind and compassionate to all beings and creatures; His Protecting Hand is over all. He is the Treasure of Excellence, the Lord of the Universe; through the Guru, He acts. God, the Inner-knower, the Searcher of hearts, is All-knowing, Unseen and Immaculately Pure. (Guru Granth Sahib, Page 300)

God is the Sustainer of the world, Merciful to the meek, the Purifier of sinners, the Transcendent Lord God. Awaken, and meditate on His Feet. (Guru Granth Sahib, Page 409)

The essence, the immaculate Lord, the Light of all – I am He and He is me – there is no difference between us. The Infinite Transcendent Lord, the Supreme Lord God – Nanak has met with Him, the Guru. (Guru Granth Sahib, Page 599)

God is omnipotent, possessing all powers; He is obtained through the Perfect, Divine Guru. (Guru Granth Sahib, Page 811)

These verses from the Guru Granth Sahib show that in Sikhi God is understood to be One, Infinite, Loving, Light, the Creator, the

Sustainer, the All-Powerful, and the All-Knowing. In Sikhi, God is often referred to as Waheguru, which means "Wonderful Guru." The term Waheguru is technically a *mantra*, which is a word or phrase that is chanted repeatedly. There are many other names for God in Sikhi, such as Satnam, which means "True Name."

History and Description of the Religion

Guru Nanak Dev was born on April 15th, 1469, in the town of Rai Bhoeki Talwandi, which is now known as Nankana Sahib, in the Punjab province of modern-day Pakistan. His family were Hindus. Nanak was a human being who was an embodiment of divine light, a celestial being, a heavenly messenger, and a teacher of humanity. Sikhs believe that the message that Guru Nanak brought came to him directly from God through the Shabad, which is God's guiding wisdom in the form of song or sound current. Guru Nanak said what God taught him to say.

Nanak showed great wisdom and knowledge from a very early age, impressing his parents and his teachers. He became fluent in Hindi, Persian, and Sanskrit. In his youth, he took to meditating in seclusion, although he did eventually marry and have children. For a time, Nanak worked as a store keeper at a granary in Sultanpur.

When Nanak was around the age of 30, he was bathing in the Baeen River when he disappeared for three days. During that time, he had a vision of God's presence in which God entrusted him to preach the Divine Name to the world. God gave him a goblet in which was nectar of the Divine Name, and the Guru drank it. Guru Nanak then conversed with God, and God confirmed Nanak's guruship. God Himself was Nanak's Guru.

When Nanak reemerged, some people saw a halo around his head. He remained silent for a day and then said, "There is no Hindu and no Muslim." This meant there was no difference between humans, but it may also have meant that Hindus and Muslims had forgotten the precepts of their religions. Nanak never asked Hindus or Muslims to become his disciples in order to be admitted into Heaven. Instead, he urged them to remain true to their religions.

Thereafter, Guru Nanak went on a few long journeys, called *udasis*, accompanied by his minstrel, Mardana, who had been born as a Muslim. Over the course of these journeys, Nanak traveled throughout India, Sri Lanka, Tibet, and the Middle East, preaching his message, performing miracles, and establishing a network of Sikh centers called *manjis*. He also discouraged people from performing rituals, he discouraged superstitions and idolatry, and he encouraged people to worship only God.

After his journeys, Guru Nanak settled in Kartarpur for the rest of his life, teaching and leading others, although sometimes he would travel within 200 miles of the city. He established, among other practices, the *langar*, which is a free communal kitchen where people can gather and eat together regardless of caste or religion. The practice of the langar continues to this day.

Before Guru Nanak passed away on September 22nd, 1539, he had appointed Angad Dev as his successor to the guruship. Guru Angad Dev meditated often, and he developed a script called *Gurmukhi*, which was used to record the Sikh scripture. Angad Dev ruled the Sikhs from the city of Khadur, and before his death in 1552, he appointed Amar Das as his successor.

Guru Amar Das ruled the Sikhs from Goindwal. He organized the manji system that had been established by Guru Nanak and continued preaching the Sikh message. Before his death, he appointed his son-in-law, Ram Das, to be his successor. Due to the devotion to the Guru on the part of Amar Das's daughter (Ram Das's wife), Bibi Bhani, Amar Das declared that the guruship would remain in their family through their descendants. This was done at the request of Bibi Bhani. Guru Amar Das passed away in 1574, and Guru Ram Das thereafter ruled the Sikhs from a new city called Ramdaspur, later called Amritsar. He also established an order of missionaries, called *masands*, to spread Sikhi. Before the death of Ram Das in 1581, he appointed his youngest son, Arjan Dev, as his successor.

Guru Arjan Dev extended Amritsar, and in that city, he oversaw the construction of the Golden Temple, a place of worship that became the center for Sikh activities. Arjan Dev traveled to preach the Sikh faith, and he also compiled the Sikh scripture, the *Adi Granth*. It was composed of hymns from the Sikh Gurus as well as hymns from Hindu saints and Muslim mystics.

There existed some power-hungry and bitter men who had animosity towards Guru Arjan Dev, and they reported slanders about him being a criminal to the Mughal emperor, Jahangir. The emperor believed the slanders because Guru Arjan Dev had given charity to a needy rival of the emperor's, who was on the run, although the Guru's charity was done out of spiritual motives as opposed to political motives. After the Guru rejected the terms that he pay a fine to the emperor and edit the Adi Granth according to the wishes of the emperor, Jahangir had Arjan Dev tortured and put to death in 1606.

Guru Arjan Dev had appointed his son, Har Gobind, as his successor, and Guru Har Gobind began to raise an army of Sikhs in order to maintain security and justice. Emperor Jahangir felt that Guru Har Gobind was undermining his authority, so he imprisoned the Guru in Gwalior Fort for about two years. When Jahangir decided to release the Guru, the Guru insisted that 52 Hindu rulers who were also imprisoned be released too. Jahangir said that anyone who could hold on to a tassel of the Guru's cloak would be freed, so the Guru had a special cloak brought to him with 52 tassels, so all of the Hindu rulers in the prison were able to be released. Emperor Jahangir eventually passed away, and his son, Emperor Shah Jahan, was fed lies about Guru Har Gobind. A skirmish took place between some Mughal soldiers and Sikh soldiers after a hunting hawk of the emperor's landed amongst the Sikhs. Thereafter, a battle was fought between the Mughals and the Sikhs, and under the leadership of Guru Har Gobind, the Sikhs were victorious. The Mughals would go on to attack the Sikhs three more times, and the Sikhs were victorious in each battle. Guru Har Gobind also founded the city of Sri Har Gobindpur, and he traveled to preach the Sikh faith, before settling at Kiratpur, where he passed away in 1644. Before his death, Guru Har Gobind appointed his grandson, Har Rai, as the next guru.

Guru Har Rai maintained the Sikh army and went on tours preaching Sikhi. He appointed his son, Har Krishen, as the next guru, before his death in 1661 at Kiratpur. Guru Har Krishen ensured that food, medicine, and clothes were given to the poor and the sick, but he soon died from smallpox in 1664. Before his death, Guru Har Krishen gave one clue about who should succeed him as guru, and the clue he spoke was, "Baba Bakale," which meant that his successor would be found in the village of Bakala. Subsequently, a man named Makhan Shah Labana discovered the next guru there when the guru spoke about a secret vow that Makhan Shah had made. The ninth guru was Tegh Bahadur, the youngest son of Guru Har Gobind.

Tegh Bahadur founded a settlement that would become a city called Anandpur, and he traveled around, preaching the Sikh religion. The Mughal emperor at that time, Aurangzeb, led a campaign in which he attempted to forcibly convert non-Muslim Indians to Islam. Guru Tegh Bahadur was arrested and brought before the emperor, and after the Guru refused to become a Muslim, Aurangzeb had him tortured and put to death in 1675. Before his death, Guru Tegh Bahadur had appointed his son, Gobind Rai, to be the next guru.

Guru Gobind Rai married and had four sons, and he emphasized purpose-driven discipline. Many of his days were given to worshipping God, instructing Sikhs, and performing physical exercises. During the time of Gobind Rai, the Sikh army grew. Guru Gobind Rai also established the *Khalsa*, the Sikh brotherhood of saint-soldiers, baptizing five disciples who volunteered, and he enjoined on them a new set of instructions. Then Guru Gobind Rai himself was baptized at his request by the five initiates, and from then on, he was known as Guru Gobind Singh. The other initiates received the surname of Singh as well, and the word *singh* means "lion." Within the next few days, about 80,000 men and women were baptized. All men received the surname of Singh, and all women received the surname of Kaur, which means "Princess," and this naming system continues amongst Sikhs to this day.

Over time, battles were fought against the Sikhs by Indian nobles and the Mughal Empire. Guru Gobind Singh led the Sikhs through this turbulent time, even withstanding the martyrdom of his four sons. The Sikh religion persisted and would continue to do so after the time of Guru Gobind Singh.

Other accomplishments of Guru Gobind Singh were that he added compositions by Guru Tegh Bahadur to the Adi Granth, and he wrote another scripture called the Dasam Granth. Later, a Mughal assassin stabbed Guru Gobind Singh in the city of Nader. The Guru killed the assassin himself, but the wound would prove fatal. Before his death, Gobind Singh appointed the Adi Granth, the Sikh scripture, as the final guru after him. From then on, instead of the Adi Granth, it would be officially, and reverently, called the *Guru Granth Sahib*. Guru Gobind Singh passed away from his wound on October 7th, 1708.

In summary, the ten human Sikh Gurus were:

1. Nanak Dev (1469-1539)
2. Angad Dev (1504-1552)

3. Amar Das (1479-1574)
4. Ram Das (1534-1581)
5. Arjan Dev (1563-1606)
6. Har Gobind (1595-1644)
7. Har Rai (1630-1661)
8. Har Krishen (1656-1664)
9. Tegh Bahadur (1621-1675)
10. Gobind Singh (1666-1708)

According to the teachings of the Sikh gurus, first there was God, existing alone and without form, before creation. Then God manifested Himself through *Nam*, the Divine Name, and then He created the world, sustaining it with His presence. All of creation came out of God and will eventually be absorbed back into God.

Sikhi teaches that there are different realms of existence, with this world being only one. After death, a soul that has not attained mukti may experience Hellish realms or Heavenly realms before being reincarnated.

God's Nam is His Divine Name, which is truth in a myriad of forms. Nam is not represented by only one word. Whatever gives insight about God is Nam, and this includes

names that refer to God. Nam also refers to the
Divine identity within each person. Some Sikhs
believe that baptism is the way to the guru, the
guru is the way to Nam, and Nam is the way to
God. However, Sikh baptism differs from
Christian baptism. In Sikhi, baptism is known as
Amrit Sanskar, a Punjabi term meaning "Nectar
Ceremony." In this ceremony, the Sikh initiate is
sprinkled with, and then consumes, *amrit*, or
nectar, which is a special sugar water, in the
presence of five Sikhs and the Guru Granth
Sahib. Once the ceremony is finished, the initiate
has officially become part of the Khalsa, the
Sikh brotherhood/sisterhood. A Sikh who has
taken amrit is called *amritdhari*. During the nectar
ceremony, and afterwards in daily life, the Sikh
wears the *Panj Kakka*, or the Five K's:

1. **Kes**: Uncut hair, representing the
   natural appearance of sainthood; Kes
   is worn in a Keski, a small turban.
2. **Kanga**: A comb that symbolizes
   combing the mind of impurities
3. **Kachha**: A warrior's shorts, which
   also represent chastity
4. **Kara**: A steel bracelet on the wrist,
   symbolizing dedication to God

5.   **Kirpan**: A blade for self-defense, symbolizing dignity, power, and unconquerable spirit

Other Sikhs do not believe that baptism is necessary, although they still believe it is beneficial as it enables one to become a visible protector of the Guru Granth Sahib. A Sikh who has not taken amrit is called *sahajdhari*.

Sikhi in practice is founded on three pillars:

1.   **Naam Japo**: Constant remembrance of God through meditation.
2.   **Kirat Karo**: Honest livelihood.
3.   **Vand Chhako**: Lovingly sharing.

Sikhs usually recite certain religious compositions, or *banis*, at three specific times of day: the Japji Sahib, the Jaap Sahib, the Tav Prasad Svaiye, the Benti Chaupai Sahib, and Anand Sahib in the morning; the Rehras Sahib after sunset; and the Kirtan Sohila Sahib at night before bed. This daily routine is called *Nitnem*. Note that the word bani is short for *Gurbani*, which refers to the teachings from the Guru Granth Sahib and the Dasam Granth.

Sikhi also forbids certain actions, including: idolatry, murdering innocents, adultery, theft, gambling, consuming intoxicants, slander, cutting one's hair (for amritdharis), and consuming *kutha* meat. Kutha meat is meat from any animal that was slaughtered in a slow and ritualistic way, such as halal and kosher meat. Meat permissible for Sikhs is called *jhatka*, and it comes from an animal that was slaughtered by severing its head, thereby killing the animal instantly.

Similarly to Sanatana Dharma and Buddhism, Sikhi teaches about the concept of *dharma*, which is natural order that can be experienced through a lack of ego. Sikhs also accept the concept of *karma*, which is the returning force of one's good or bad actions. Another similarity between Sanatana Dharma, Buddhism, and Sikhi is that there is no concept of an overall "Devil."

Sikh scholars formed the SGPC (Shiromani Gurdwara Parbandhak Committee), which administers certain gurdwaras in India. They produced a code of conduct for Sikhs in 1950 called the *Sikh Rehat Maryada*, and it defines a

Sikh as "any human being who faithfully believes in:

1. One immortal Being

2. Ten gurus, from Guru Nanak to Guru Gobind Singh

3. The Guru Granth Sahib

4. The utterances and teachings of the ten gurus

5. The baptism bequeathed by the tenth guru

6. And who does not owe allegiance to any other religion"

There have also evolved Sikh sects that differ from Orthodox Sikhi, and these include Nirankari and Namdhari. They differ from Orthodox Sikhi in that they recognize additional human gurus.

Significant Times throughout the Year

Significant times in Sikhi include, but are not limited to, the following:

Vaisakhi: This day commemorates the forming of the Khalsa by Guru Gobind Singh.

Sikhism

Bandi Chhor Divas: This day commemorates the release of Guru Har Gobind from prison.

The Gurpurab of Guru Nanak Dev: This day commemorates the birthday of Guru Nanak Dev.

The Gurpurab of Guru Gobind Singh: This day commemorates the birthday of Guru Gobind Singh.

Virtues in Sikhi

Anger Management

Cruelty, material attachment, greed and anger are the four rivers of fire. Falling into them, one is burned, O Nanak! One is saved only by holding tight to good deeds. (Guru Granth Sahib, Page 147)

Within this body dwell the five thieves: sexual desire, anger, greed, emotional attachment and egotism. They plunder the Nectar, but the self-willed manmukh (i.e., follower of desire) does not realize it; no one hears his complaint. (Guru Granth Sahib, Page 600)

Fareed, answer evil with goodness; do not fill your mind with anger. (Guru Granth Sahib, Page 1381)

Forgiveness

Where there is greed, there is death. Where there is forgiveness, there is God Himself. (Guru Granth Sahib, Page 1372)

Gratitude

In the most horrible hell, there is terrible pain and suffering. It is the place of the ungrateful. (Guru Granth Sahib, Page 315)

Humility

Sweetness and humility, O Nanak, are the essence of virtue and goodness. (Guru Granth Sahib, Page 470)

Kindness

Show kindness and mercy to all beings, and realize that the Lord is pervading everywhere; this is the way of life of the enlightened soul, the supreme swan. (Guru Granth Sahib, Page 508)

Sikhism

Love

Sing, and listen, and let your mind be filled with love. Your pain shall be sent far away, and peace shall come to your home. (Guru Granth Sahib, Page 2)

The God-conscious being looks upon all alike, like the wind, which blows equally upon the king and the poor beggar. (Guru Granth Sahib, Page 272)

Patience

Let patience be your purpose in life; implant this within your being. (Guru Granth Sahib, Page 1384)

The Symbol of the Religion

The symbol that is often associated with Sikhi is called the *Khanda*. The double-edged sword in the center symbolizes divine knowledge that separates truth from falsehood. The circle around the double-edged sword in the center symbolizes the perfection and eternality of God. The two curved swords on either side symbolize the equal emphasis that a Sikh must place on worldly strength (*miri*) and spiritual strength (*piri*).

Chapter 7: Miracles and Spiritual Experiences

Introduction

Accounts of spiritual experiences, and by extension, miracles, exist in every major religion. Some adherents of particular faiths regard miracles as "proof" for the validity of their religion. Other religious adherents may acknowledge the existence of miracles, yet they entirely disregard these phenomena as proof for their religion, dismissing them as a simple byproduct of following the founder's message. After all, to them the message of the religion is significantly more important than any dazzling wonders performed by the founder or sages of the religion. They believe that personal mystical experiences or simple logic serve as evidence for their religion's validity.

Nevertheless, miracles are important to many individuals because they may be viewed as a link to a higher power as well as an unseen realm. Perhaps the shared accounts of miraculous events from a diverse array of faith traditions can help bridge the gap of understanding that many people have regarding different faith traditions.

But first of all, what does one mean by the term "miracle"? Definitions of the word "miracle" include the following:

- "An effect or extraordinary event in the physical world that surpasses all known human or natural powers and is ascribed to a supernatural cause." [from *Dictionary.com*]

- "An extraordinary event manifesting divine intervention in human affairs." [from *Merriam-Webster.com*]

- "An event that appears inexplicable by the laws of nature and so is held to be supernatural in origin or an act of

Miracles and Spiritual Experiences

God." [from *The American Heritage
Dictionary of the English Language*]

In other words, miracles are events that
should not normally occur because we cannot
explain them with physical laws. Despite this,
miracle stories exist in all of the major faith
traditions, be they Abrahamic (Judaism,
Christianity, and Islam) or Dharmic
(Hinduism, Buddhism, and Sikhism). A skeptic
may argue that miracles are just myths from
bygone eras, used to manipulate the
imaginations of naïve followers. After all, most
of the popular miracle stories are from long
ago, when humanity was generally more
superstitious. Then again, a believer may argue
that these stories are unique because they
center around unique individuals. For example,
if a man truly had a message from God, then
perhaps it would make sense for God to
support that man even through extraordinary
means. Whether one accepts the skeptic's
assessment or the believer's assessment is not
the point of this chapter. Instead, the focus will
be the fact that different pathways to the same
Source, which many call God, have similar tales
of extraordinary wonders. No religion has

more "objective" miracles than another. And no religion has more "miraculous" miracles than another.

Miracles in Sanatana Dharma (Hinduism)

In ancient times, Vishnu incarnated into human form as Krishna to restore dharma, bringing order to the world. Krishna was raised by foster parents in a village of cowherders in northern India. On one occasion, as is told in the Puranas, the god Indra became angry with the villagers for ceasing to give offerings to him, instead giving them to the mountain Govardhana. Indra then afflicted them with tumultuous rain, but Krishna raised the mountain over the villagers, using it as an umbrella to shield them from Indra's wrath. When Indra realized that he could not overcome Krishna, he stopped the assault.

Millennia later, the Hindu saint Chaitanya Mahaprabhu (1486 – 1534 C.E.) was capable of healing the sick. This included an incident during which he healed a leper named Vasudeva. Chaitanya also temporarily restored life to the deceased child of a fellow saint, Srivasa Thakura.

More recently, a Hindu yogi known as Paramahansa Yogananda recorded in his famous *Autobiography of a Yogi* a tale told to him by his guru, Sri Yukteswar. The latter recounted that a friend of his named Rama had died of Asiatic cholera, but he was then returned to life through Sri Yukteswar's guru, Lahiri Mahasaya (1828 – 1895 C.E.). In a separate incident, a Hindu saint known as Bengali Baba was reported to have brought back to life a prince of Bhawal, in India.

Miracles in Sanatana Dharma are not limited to only healings and reviving the dead, and one may find a plethora of different wonders attributed to various sages. For example, a saint known as Shree Maa of Kamakhya has been reported to be able to influence weather. And around the 8th century C.E., Adi Shankaracharya saved his guru, Govinda Bhagavatpada, from a flood by consecrating a bowl with a sacred mantra. The flood water miraculously flowed into the bowl.

Miracles in Judaism

The Tanakh (i.e., the Hebrew Bible) contains many stories of miracles all throughout the text. Abraham's wife Sarah was barren, and she was quite old, when God allowed them to miraculously conceive Isaac. Hundreds of years later, God gave Moses certain signs to perform in front of people. Among these signs were the staff of Moses turning into a snake, Moses's hand turning white with scales after putting it in his bosom, and the turning of water from the Nile into blood after pouring it on dry ground. The miracles of the entire nation of the Israelites being saved from Pharaoh and thereafter hearing the voice of God at Mount Sinai have already been related earlier in the chapter on Judaism.

Several miracles also happened during the time of Moses's successor, Joshua. One of them was when, at Joshua's word, the sun stood still in the sky for a whole day while the Israelites fought the Amorites in Canaan.

Centuries later, the Prophet Elijah predicted a drought to King Ahab. Many other miracles occurred through that prophet. When Elijah was fleeing from the wrath of Ahab and his wife, Queen Jezebel, he stayed with a widow and her child at Zarephath. Through the prophet, God multiplied the amount of flour and oil that the widow had so that it was enough to sustain the three of them throughout the drought. Later, the widow's child died, but God restored the child to life through Elijah. Eventually there was a contest between Elijah, representing God, and 450 prophets of Baal on Mount Carmel. There, God miraculously sent a fire to consume Elijah's offering of a bull. No such thing was done for the offering of the prophets of Baal. Towards the end of his time in the world, Elijah divided the water of the Jordan River in order to cross it with his successor, Elisha, who would go on to perform several miracles himself. One miracle of Elisha was that he instructed Naaman, the commander of the army of the king of Aram, to bathe in the Jordan River in order for Naaman to cure his leprosy. The Tanakh records this occurring as Elisha had prescribed.

Many miracles are said to have occurred in Jewish tradition outside of the Tanakh as well. In the 1st century C.E., Rabbi Hanina ben Dosa healed the sick child of Rabbi Gamaliel through prayer. Rabbi Israel ben Eliezer (1698 – 1760 C.E.), known as the Baal Shem Tov or the "Besht," is regarded as the founder of a Jewish movement called Hasidism. The Besht was said to have performed several miracles, including healing sick people and restoring a blind boy's sight.

Miracles in Buddhism

There are several narrations of Gautama Buddha performing miracles. He was reported to have defeated a snake deity of the Jatilas, a community of renunciates, through meditation in a battle of smoke and fire. Then the Buddha miraculously caused 500 pieces of firewood to split, burst into flame, and extinguish, all in front of the Jatilas. Lastly, the Buddha controlled a flood that afflicted the Jatilas, and he rose in the air during that incident. On another occasion, the Buddha calmed an angry elephant named Nalagiri in the town of Rajagaha. The Buddha also allegedly ascended into the sky in front of his father, the leader of the Sakya tribe, before descending back to earth.

The Buddhist nun, Gotami, who was also Siddhartha Gautama's aunt, was said to have been able to walk through walls and through the sky. Similarly, another disciple of the Buddha's named Pindola Bharadvaja flew around a city three times on one occasion. And the famous Indian emperor, Ashoka (c. 304 – 232 B.C.E.), was said to have converted to Buddhism after witnessing miracles performed by a Buddhist named Samudra. Samudra had survived being in an iron cauldron under which a fire was burning. When it had no effect on him, Samudra flew into the sky and shone in front of Ashoka. He thereafter explained the Dharma to the emperor.

Miracles in Christianity

Miracle stories abound in the New Testament and in other Christian writings.

Several miracles of Jesus have already been mentioned in the chapter on Christianity. Jesus was known to heal the sick, including several lepers and blind people. He was also reported to have raised back to life a dead man named Lazarus. The gospels, which are the narrative accounts of Jesus's life contained within the New Testament, also relate how Jesus turned water into wine at a wedding. On a separate occasion, Jesus walked on water, and in another incident Jesus calmed a storm. In yet another famous story, Jesus was able to adequately feed a crowd of 5,000 people from five small barley loaves and two small fish.

The Book of Acts in the New Testament similarly relates how the Apostle Peter and the Apostle Paul each were able to heal people. Hundreds of years later, Saint Athanasius, who died in 373 C.E., wrote about Saint Antony, who accurately informed two parents about an ailment that their daughter had. Antony also accurately predicted that the daughter would be healed. Pope Gregory the Great, who died in 604 C.E., narrated a story about a pious Christian monk named Libertinus who revived a woman's dead son on the way to Ravenna.

There also existed a Christian saint by the name of Cuthbert, who died in 687 C.E. Information about him is found in the writings of the Venerable Bede. Cuthbert allegedly healed the sick, performed successful exorcisms, and caused crops to grow in inhospitable areas. Much later, during the 19th century in North America, the Mormon prophet Joseph Smith (1805 – 1844 C.E.) was said to be able to heal the sick.

Miracles in Islam

There are numerous miracles attributed to the Prophet Muhammad. The Muslim scholar Al-Ghazali (c. 1058 – 1111 C.E.) listed many of them in his book, *The Revival of the Religious Sciences* (in Arabic: *Ihya 'Ulum Ad-Din*). A contemporary work that expounds on the miracles of Muhammad is *The Final Prophet* by Mohammad Elshinawy. These later books gather reports of the miracles of Muhammad from the hadiths and the sirah (i.e., biography) of the Prophet. A few miracles are also referenced in the Qur'an.

Some miracles of Muhammad include the multiplication of food in the house of Jabir ibn 'Abdullah, in the house of Abu Talhah, and during the digging of the trench (Al-Khandaq). Muhammad was also reported to have provided water from small amounts for hundreds of men at a time, in places such as Al-Hudaybiyah and Tabuk. The Prophet also foretold the martyrdom of several of his companions, including 'Umar, 'Uthman, and 'Ammar ibn Yasir. On one occasion, he was asked to pray for rain, and it rained profusely. Later he was asked to pray for the rain to stop, and it stopped. Muhammad also healed people in some instances. For example, he cured the eyes of his companion 'Ali at Khaybar, and he cured another companion's eye after it fell out. And the Qur'an states that at the Battle of Badr, which was the first major militaristic engagement between the Muslims of Medina and the Quraysh of Mecca, God sent thousands of angels to assist the Muslims in battle.

Later Muslims throughout history have also been reported to perform miracles. The Prophet Muhammad's companion, 'Umar ibn

Al-Khattab, once miraculously advised a Muslim commander named Sariyah ibn Zanim during battle from an entirely different city based on a vision of the battle. Hundreds of years later, the scholar Ibn Taymiyyah (1263 – 1328 C.E.) was reported to have great intuition and predicted losses and victories between the Muslim communities and the invading Tatars.

There is a mystical tradition of Islam known as Sufism, and one Sufi saint, Habib Al-Ajami (c. 8th century C.E.), was reported to have performed miracles that included him walking on water. And a scholar named 'Abdullah ibn Al-Mubarak, who lived in the 8th century C.E., was said to have prayed for a certain blind man to be cured, and the blind man's sight was restored.

Miracles in Sikhi (Sikhism)

Many miracles are attributed to Guru Nanak, the founder of Sikhi. When Nanak began his travels, one of his first stops was at Saidpur, now known as Eminabad. There lived in Saidpur a poor carpenter named Lalo, who was righteous and loving. The chief of the town, Malik Bhago, was corrupt and exploited the poor. After Guru Nanak initially rejected Malik Bhago's invitation to meet, Nanak later agreed to see him. At that meeting, Nanak held a loaf of Malik Bhago's bread and a loaf of Lalo's bread, and he squeezed each one. Milk dripped out of Lalo's bread, but blood dripped out of Malik Bhago's bread. This convinced Malik Bhago to change his life for the better.

During his journeys, Guru Nanak briefly stayed at a place called Hasan Abdal. It was there that an arrogant man named Bawa Wali Qandhari rolled a large rock down a hill toward Guru Nanak in order to crush him. The Guru simply raised his hand and the rock stopped at it. Bawa Wali Qandhari recognized the miracle and humbled himself before the Guru. To this day, the rock is there with the imprint of Guru Nanak's hand, at the gurdwara called Panja Sahib.

At one point in his travels, Guru Nanak went to Mecca. While he was in the sanctuary around the Ka'bah, he was lying down with his feet pointing towards the Ka'bah. A Muslim named

Jiwan kicked him and chastised him for pointing his feet towards the House of God. Nanak replied, "Turn my feet in the direction where God is not." At this, Jiwan shifted the Guru's feet, but the Ka'bah shifted too, and people there recognized Nanak as a holy man. (It is important to note that Jiwan's objection to Nanak's feet pointing towards the Ka'bah was a cultural objection. Such an objection is not based in the Qur'an or authentic hadiths. Furthermore, God does not literally reside within the Ka'bah. It is called the House of God because it is a place where God is worshipped. Perhaps these were points that Guru Nanak wished to remind Jiwan of.)

Other Sikh gurus were reported to have performed miracles as well. Guru Arjan Dev bore his tortures with miraculous patience and serenity until his death. Guru Har Krishen wondrously healed lepers and those afflicted with smallpox, and he enabled a mute illiterate man named Chhaju to give a Hindu brahmin explanations about the Bhagavad Gita. And Guru Gobind Singh was also reported to have caused a leper to be healed after he pushed the leper into a pool.

Boasted Miracles

Some zealous followers of certain religions attempt to magnify the significance of reported miraculous events. For example, Jewish tradition states that approximately 3 million people, the *entire* nation of the Israelites at that time, heard the voice of God speak to them at Mount Sinai. The Apostle Paul relates that Jesus appeared to over 500 Christians after he was resurrected from death (1 Corinthians 15:6). And according to some companions of the Prophet Muhammad, one of whom was 'Abdullah ibn Mas'ud, on one occasion in Mecca, some people of the Quraysh came to Muhammad and requested a sign. At this, the moon split in two, part of it went towards a mountain, and Muhammad said, "Bear witness." Afterwards, the moon became whole again. Presumably, the entire tribe of Quraysh, consisting of hundreds of people, would have been able to see the moon being split, especially since none of the disbelievers were recorded to have raised objections to the tale of this miracle, and this miracle is referenced in the Qur'an (54:1). The splitting of the moon is related in Sahih Al-Bukhari, Hadith 3869 and in Sahih Muslim, Hadith 2800.

Millions of people hearing the voice of God? Hundreds of people witnessing a resurrected Christ? Hundreds of people witnessing the moon being split in two? These are certainly significant claims. However, we must not let our subjectivity get the better of us. These alleged events were all written in their standard forms long after they were said to have taken place – decades or even centuries after. Much may become exaggerated and many may become confused by rumors in such an amount of time. Even good people who speak with sincerity can become mislead by a profound rumor. Furthermore, we do not have millions, thousands, hundreds, or even tens of *individual* testimonies about these miracles. We only have the testimonies of a few sources, one or two for each event – the Torah, Paul, the Qur'an, and a hadith. One source saying that many people heard or witnessed something does not necessarily mean that it actually happened, especially if that source cannot be independently corroborated. I wish to assure the reader that I am not saying that each of these miracles did not occur. Furthermore, I say this not to disparage those who sincerely believe in these miracles, but I say this only in an attempt to help people realize that one religion's miracles are not necessarily better or more reliable than another.

Spiritual Experiences

In addition to miracles, many people rely on personal spiritual experiences as evidence for the validity of their religion. There are many anecdotes, old and new, about visions of figures such as Jesus, Muhammad, Gautama Buddha, and other religious figures. However, one may argue that these spiritual experiences contradict one another. After all, how can one person have a vision confirming Jesus Christ as their Lord and Savior while another person has a vision in which Muhammad is confirmed to be God's final messenger, and still another person may have a vision confirming Siddhartha Gautama as the Buddha?

A materialist may assert that one simply hallucinates a particular religious figure based on their social conditioning. For example, those in Christian countries have visions of Jesus, and those in Muslim countries have visions of Muhammad. This may be partly true, but it ignores the fact that now and then a story may surface of a Muslim who has a vision of Jesus or a Christian who has a vision of Muhammad. Both types of incidents have been recorded, and examples may be found in the book *The Source and Significance of Coincidences* by Sharon Hewitt Rawlette, PhD. A spiritual person with a universalist mindset may attempt to reconcile these visions with the notion that God (which one may refer to as "Source," "the Absolute Reality," or anything else) reaches out to individuals based on their personal needs. Whatever comforts a person, or whatever path will help a person, is how God will approach that person. This is, of course, a hypothesis that is unable to be tested in this life, at least as far as we know.

Nevertheless, it is clear that spiritual experiences can be found in all religions. An example of this may be displayed in the life of the famous Hindu saint Ramakrishna (1836 – 1886 C.E.). Ramakrishna was essentially a spiritual prodigy who could enter high states of consciousness. He was a devotee of the Goddess Kali and would have visions of her. However, a time came when Ramakrishna embraced Islam. During this time, the saint practiced the religion piously, avoiding the Hindu murtis and performing salah five times a day. After three days, Ramakrishna had a vision of the Prophet Muhammad dissolving into God, upon which Ramakrishna went into intense ecstasy. Thereafter, he returned to his Hindu lifestyle. Later, Ramakrishna briefly embraced Christianity until he went into ecstasy upon seeing a vision of Jesus merging into his heart. Ramakrishna would go on to spend the rest of his life as a Hindu devotee of Kali, but he would know that Islam and Christianity were both valid paths to God as well.

What we can learn from Ramakrishna, and others like him, is that all faith traditions can lead to feelings of truth and ecstasy. This fact alone does not necessarily mean that they are all correct, but it also does not mean that they are all wrong. Miracle stories and spiritual experiences, in and of themselves, simply do not provide enough evidence to make a religion exclusively true. Virtue may be a better indicator of a religion's validity, and regardless of what ideology leads to God or enlightenment, virtue may be the most important commonality among all major ideologies.

Conclusion

The major religions of the world indeed differ ideologically and ritualistically, as has been detailed in the preceding chapters, but differences can be interesting. Through studying what makes each religious path unique, we come to understand one another, and such understanding may reflect positively in people's interactions with each other. Some people tend to fear the unknown, so in this case, knowledge may dissipate fear, and if one stops fearing others based on their different beliefs, then this is a step closer toward respecting others, and everyone wants to be respected.

However, an additional understanding of underlying similarities may be essential to uniting humanity in the spirit of love, or at least tolerance. Love and tolerance foster peace, and peace leads to a happier, healthier state of being. Perhaps the most significant similarities of the world religions lie in their virtues, some of which, as I have attempted to show, are essentially identical. Imagine if all people implemented anger management, forgiveness, gratitude, humility, kindness, love, and patience in their lives; the world might be a better place. If a person sincerely adheres to any of the religious paths described in this book, these virtues might be shown through that person. Some people use religion as a tool to perform immoral actions, but one should not judge a religion based on the atrocities committed by its so-called followers. One must instead judge a religion based on its founder and its source material (i.e., its scripture or scriptures).

Furthermore, most religions not only share certain virtuous teachings, but they also share a belief in God. While there are differences in belief about God amongst the major religions, the *essential* qualities of God are indistinguishable. Hindus, Jews, Christians, Muslims, and Sikhs can all agree that God is One, Infinite, Loving, Light, the Creator, the Sustainer, the All-Powerful, and the All-Knowing. These are important commonalities for people to acknowledge. Whether God is referred to as Brahman, Ishvara, Adonai,

Elohim, HaShem, Abba, Allah, Rabb, Waheguru, or Satnam, God has the same essential qualities. Moreover, if God is loving towards people, then people should also be loving towards people, and in doing so they may become closer to God. This is one reason why love has been included as one of the virtues focused on within this book.

Even though we may not share the same prayers, many of us share a belief in God. And even though we may not all share a belief in God, we can all still share the same virtues.

I wish peace and guidance to all who read this.

Acknowledgements

I would like to thank my parents (Paula and Ayub), Imam Adam, Andy, Jeremy, Julie, Dr. Murty, Ek Ong Kaar Kaur, Maninder Singh, and Dr. Kramer for their helpful reviews, suggestions, discussions, and encouragements.

Bibliography

Online Bibliography

Acharya, Dharma Pravartaka. " Perfect Questions, Perfect Answers - Addressing the Facts and Myths of Sanatana Dharma." *Dharma Central*, 2017, https://dharmacentral.com/tpost/emk55lk9y 1-perfect-questions-perfect-answers-addres. Accessed 20 June 2025.

Ahuja, Ravi. "5 Most Popular Hindu Festivals." *Medium*, 04 August 2017, https://medium.com/@meraviahuja/5-most-popular-hindu-festivals-bfe0b5cd3ef0. Accessed 04 September 2024.

Allard, Syama. "5 things to know about Om." *Hindu American Foundation*, 16 July 2020, https://www.hinduamerican.org/blog/5-things-to-know-about-om. Accessed 05 February 2024.

"Anguttara Nikaya: Book of the Twos." Translated by Thanissaro Bhikkhu. *Suttacentral.net*, https://suttacentral.net/an2.32-41/en/thanissaro?lang=en&reference=none&highlight=false. Accessed 06 February 2024.

Baron, Doniel. "Insights into the Hebrew Language: The Word "Jew"." *Aish.com*, https://aish.com/48955566/. Accessed 05 February 2024.

"Basic Passages 9: The Discourse on Love." Translated by Bhikkhu Sujato. *Suttacentral.net*, 2020, https://suttacentral.net/kp9/en/sujato?lang=en&layout=plain&reference=none&notes=asterisk&highlight=false&script=latin. Accessed 06 February 2024.

"Buddhists celebrate birth of Gautama Buddha." *History.com*, 09 February 2010, https://www.history.com/this-day-in-history/buddhists-celebrate-birth-of-gautama-buddha. Accessed 13 February 2024.

Coopersmith, Nechemia. "Did God Speak at Sinai?" Aish.com, https://aish.com/did_god_speak_at_sinai/. Accessed 10 June 2025.

Davidson, Baruch S. "What Are Angels?" *Chabad.org*, https://www.chabad.org/library/article_cdo/aid/692875/jewish/What-Are-Angels.htm. Accessed 12 February 2024.

Dhillon, K.S. "The Granthi." *SikhNet.com*, 02 July 2014, https://www.sikhnet.com/news/granthi. Accessed 18 September 2024.

Eisen, Yosef. "The History of the Mishnah." *Chabad.org*, https://www.chabad.org/library/article_cdo/aid/2714790/jewish/The-History-of-the-Mishnah.htm. Accessed 05 February 2024.

"Gayatri Mantra – A Universal Prayer." *Sri Sathya Sai International Organization*, https://www.sathyasai.org/devotional/gayatri#:~:text=General%20meaning%3A%20We%20meditate%20on,divine%20light%20illumine%20our%20intellect.. Accessed 06 February 2024.

"Gemara: The Essence of the Talmud." *My Jewish Learning*, https://www.myjewishlearning.com/article/gemara-the-essence-of-the-talmud/. Accessed 05 February 2024.

"Grass and Sticks." Translated by Bhikkhu Sujato. *Suttacentral.net*, 2018, https://suttacentral.net/sn15.1/en/sujato?lang=en&layout=plain&reference=none&notes=asterisk&highlight=false&script=latin. Accessed 24 February 2024.

Guru Granth Sahib, The. Khalsa Consensus Translation. https://www.sikhitothemax.org/. Accessed 06 February 2024.

"Hinduism 101: Everything you need to know about caste, Varna & Jati." *YouTube*, uploaded by The Festival of Bharat, 21 April 2023, https://www.youtube.com/watch?v=iVxUu7LycZc. Accessed 23 August 2024.

"Hindu Religious Worker Definitions." *Hindu American Foundation*, https://www.hinduamerican.org/hindu-religious-worker-definitions. Accessed 18 September 2024.

"History of Christianity from an Academic Point of View." *YouTube*, uploaded by UsefulCharts, 15 September 2023, https://www.youtube.com/watch?v=8q6FUlay-M8&t=10350s. Accessed 17 June 2025.

"Jewish Denominations Explained." *YouTube*, uploaded by UsefulCharts, 04 August 2023,

https://www.youtube.com/watch?v=AsBglu
FGz7Y&t=1823s&ab_channel=UsefulCharts.
Accessed 11 February 2024.

"Joseph Smith – Miracles." *Joseph Smith Foundation*,
https://josephsmithfoundation.org/joseph-
smith-miracles/. Accessed 17 June 2025.

"Karaamaat (miracles) that happened to some
righteous people." Islamqa, 20 May 2012,
https://islamqa.info/en/answers/175604/kar
aamaat-(miracles)-that-happened-to-some-
righteous-people. Accessed 10 June 2025.

Khalsa, Harijot Singh. "Can Sikhs Do
Miracles?" SikhNet, 26 June 2023,
https://www.sikhnet.com/news/can-sikhs-
do-miracles. Accessed 10 June 2025.

"Long Discourses 13: Experts in the Three
Vedas." Translated by Bhikkhu Sujato.
Suttacentral.net, 2018,
https://suttacentral.net/dn13/en/sujato?lang
=en&layout=plain&reference=none&notes=
asterisk&highlight=false&script=latin.
Accessed 06 February 2024.

Lopez, Donald S. "Buddha." *Encyclopedia
Britannica*, 2 Feb. 2024,
https://www.britannica.com/biography/Bud

dha-founder-of-Buddhism. Accessed 13
February 2024.

McLeod, William Hewat. "Sikhism."
Encyclopedia Britannica, 25 January 2024,
https://www.britannica.com/topic/Sikhism.
Accessed 11 February 2024.

Posner, Menachem. "The Ten
Commandments." *Chabad.org*,
https://www.chabad.org/library/article_cdo/
aid/2896/jewish/What-Are-the-Ten-
Commandments.htm. Accessed 05 February
2024.

Ramblings of a Sikh. "Sikhism Vs. Sikhi."
SikhNet.com, 14 September 2015,
https://www.sikhnet.com/news/sikhism-vs-
sikhi. Accessed 09 March 2024.

"Religious Emblems." *Sikhs.org*,
https://www.sikhs.org/khanda.htm. Accessed
05 February 2024.

Rich, Tracey. "Aseret ha-Dibrot: The Ten
Commandments." *Jewfaq.org*,
https://www.jewfaq.org/10_commandments.
Accessed 06 February 2024.

Rich, Tracey. "Olam Ha-Ba: The Afterlife."
Jewfaq.org,

https://www.jewfaq.org/afterlife#Resurrecti on. Accessed 05 February 2024.

Rich, Tracey. "Signs and Symbols." *Jewfaq.org*, https://www.jewfaq.org/signs_and_symbols. Accessed 05 February 2024.

"SATAN: What the Bible Really Teaches About the Devil –Reply2 One for Israel Messianic Jews for Jesus." *YouTube*, uploaded by Jews for Judaism, 23 August 2013, https://www.youtube.com/watch?v=KGNA OZTXkac&ab_channel=JewsforJudaism. Accessed 12 February 2024.

Shurpin, Yehuda. "Can Angels Sin?" *Chabad.org*, https://www.chabad.org/library/article_cdo/ aid/1055341/jewish/Can-Angels-Sin.htm. Accessed 12 February 2024.

"SOME MIRACLES OF SRI CAITANYA MAHA PRABHU!" Krishna Today, https://krishnatoday.com/miracles-of-sri-caitanya/. Accessed 10 June 2025.

Spiro, Ken. "History Crash Course #26: The Great Assembly." *Aish.com*, https://aish.com/48939022/. Accessed 06 February 2024.

Spitzer, Jeffrey. "The Noahide Laws." *My Jewish Learning*, https://www.myjewishlearning.com/article/the-noahide-laws/. Accessed 06 February 2024.

Thakkar, Arjun. "Hinduism isn't just worshipping cows." *The Michigan Daily*, 21 April 2019, https://www.michigandaily.com/michigan-in-color/hinduism-isnt-just-worshipping-cows/. Accessed 13 February 2024.

"The Importance of Cow Protection." *YouTube*, uploaded by DharmaNation, 31 August 2023, https://www.youtube.com/watch?v=bmo4B77R2Rw&ab_channel=DharmaNation. Accessed 13 February 2024.

"The Scriptures of Sanatana Dharma." *YouTube*, uploaded by DharmaNation, 16 October 2011, https://www.youtube.com/watch?v=6sgj5MdRFx4. Accessed 23 June 2025.

"THE STAR OF DAVID: Origins of an Ancient Symbol – Rabbi Michael Skobac – Jews for Judaism." *YouTube*, uploaded by Jews for Judaism, 14 July 2019, https://www.youtube.com/watch?v=_tGNW

dYLUaY&ab_channel=JewsforJudaism.
Accessed 06 February 2024.

"The 7 Noahide Laws: Universal Morality."
Chabad.org,
https://www.chabad.org/library/article_cdo/
aid/62221/jewish/The-7-Noahide-Laws-
Universal-Morality.htm. Accessed 06 February
2024.

Tripitaka, The.
https://suttacentral.net/?lang=en. Accessed
06 February 2024.

"Two authentic Ahaadeeth about angel
Meekaa'eel (Michael)." *Islamweb.net*, 25
November 2012,
https://www.islamweb.net/en/fatwa/191645/t
wo-authentic-ahaadeeth-about-angel-
meekaaeel-michael. Accessed 11 February
2024.

"Varna, jati & ashrama: an idiot-proof
explanation on what caste is NOT | Nilesh
Nilkanth Oak ji." *YouTube*, uploaded by The
Festival of Bharat, 13 April 2021.
https://www.youtube.com/watch?v=8HcBCadU
Fxw&t=5s. Accessed 23 August 2024.

Wang, Celina. "What is the Dharma Wheel?
Meaning and Significance in Buddhism."

Buddha & Karma, 21 October 2022,
https://buddhaandkarma.com/blogs/guide/d
harma-wheel-meaning. Accessed 05 February
2024.

"What are Yuga, Maha Yuga, Manavantara,
Kalpa, Ahotram? Fully Explained." *YouTube*,
uploaded by The Hindu Saga, 14 January 2022,
https://www.youtube.com/watch?v=Svq0kF3
pdgY. Accessed 03 September 2024.

"What is Nitnem?" *basicsofsikhi.com*, 08 March
2022,
https://www.basicsofsikhi.com/post/what-
is-nitnem. Accessed 09 March 2024.

"What is the story behind 51 Shakti Peeth |
51 body parts of Goddess Shakti | Aadi
Peruku." *YouTube*, uploaded by Temples
India, 01 July 2023,
https://www.youtube.com/watch?v=4VGw
DkB-1bU&ab_channel=TemplesIndia.
Accessed 06 September 2024.

"What Is The Tetragrammaton?" *My Jewish
Learning*,
https://www.myjewishlearning.com/article/t
he-tetragrammaton/. Accessed 06 February
2024.

"WHY JEWS DON'T BELIEVE IN JESUS
• Why Jesus is Not the Jewish Messiah • Julius
Ciss Jews for Judaism." *YouTube*, uploaded by
Jews for Judaism, 09 January 2021,
https://www.youtube.com/watch?v=ep8jcz_
hk_A&ab_channel=JewsforJudaism.
Accessed 06 February 2024.

World Population Review. World Population
Review, 2024,
https://worldpopulationreview.com/country-
rankings/religion-by-country. Accessed 07
February 2024.

World Population Review. World Population
Review, 2024,
https://worldpopulationreview.com/country-
rankings/sikhism-by-country. Accessed 07
February 2024.

Textual Bibliography

Ali, Syed Bashir. *Scholars of Hadith*. IQRA'
Educational Foundation, 2003.

al-Khudri Bak al-Bajuri, Muhammad. *The History
of the Four Caliphs*. Turath Publishing, 2012.

Al-Mubarakpuri, Safi-ur-Rahman. *Ar-Raheeq
Al-Makhtum*. Darussalam, 1979. 1996.

Bank, Richard. *The Everything Judaism Book*. Adams Media Corporation, 2002.

Bhagavad Gita, The. Translated by Eknath Easwaran, The Blue Mountain Center of Meditation: Nilgiri Press, 1985. 2007.

Bodhi, Bhikkhu, editor. *In the Buddha's Words: An Anthology of Discourses from the Pali Canon*. Wisdom Publications, Inc., 2005.

Brown, Jonathan A.C. *Hadith: Muhammad's Legacy in the Medieval and Modern World*. Oneworld Publications, 2010.

Clear Qur'an, The. Translated by Mustafa Khattab, Book of Signs Foundation, 2016.

Cohen, Abraham. *Everyman's Talmud*. Schocken Books Inc. 1949. 1975.

Dhammapada, The. Translated by Ananda Maitreya, Parallax Press. 1988. 1995.

Holy Bible, The. New Internation Version, Zondervan, 2011.

Holy Vedas, The. Translated by Pandit Satyakam Vidyalankar, Penguin Random House India, 1972. 2020.

Isma'il ibn 'Umar ibn Kathir. *Tafsir Ibn Kathir (Abridged)*. Darussalam, 2003.

Johnsen, Linda. *The Complete Idiot's Guide to Hinduism*. 2nd ed., Penguin Group, 2009.

Lings, Martin. *Muhammad: His Life Based on the Earliest Sources*. Inner Traditions, 1983. 2006.

Muhammad ibn Isma'il Al-Bukhari. *Sahih Al-Bukhari*. Translated by Muhammad Muhsin Khan, Darussalam, 1997.

Muslim ibn Al-Ḥajjāj. *Sahih Muslim*. Translated by Nasiruddin al-Khattab, Darussalam, 2007.

Nayak, Satyarth. *Mahagatha: 100 Tales from the Puranas*. HarperCollins Publishers, 2022.

Nesbitt, Eleanor. *Sikhism: A Very Short Introduction*. Oxford University Press. 2005. 2016.

Pramananda, Swamini, and Sri Dhira Chaitanya. *Purna Vidya: Puja & Prayers*. Purna Vidya Trust, 2000.

Rawlette, Sharon Hewitt. *The Source and Significance of Coincidences*. 2019.

Sach, Jacky. *The Everything Buddhism Book*. Adams Media, 2003.

Sandhu, Gian Singh. *Who Are The Sikhs?*. Archway Publishing, 2023.

Sikh Gurus. Om Books International, 2013.

Sikh Religion. Sikh Missionary Center, 1990.

Tanakh, The. Translated by The Jewish Publication Society, Jewish Publication Society, 1985.

Upanishads, The. Translated by Eknath Easwaran, The Blue Mountain Center of Meditation: Nilgiri Press, 1987. 2007.

Wagner, Richard. *Christianity for Dummies*. Wiley Publishing, Inc., 2004.

Woodward, Kenneth L. *The Book of Miracles*. Touchstone, 2000.

Wylen, Stephen. *The Jews in the Time of Jesus*. Paulist Press, 1996.

Yahya ibn Sharaf An-Nawawi. *Riyad As-Salihin*. Translated by Dr. Muhammad Amin Abu Usamah Al-Arabi bin Razduq, Darussalam, 2003.

Yogananda, Paramahansa. *Autobiography of a Yogi*. Self-Realization Fellowship, 1946. 2007.